100 + Top 1
Setting Up
Own Business

Written by

Ian Munro

and

Jacqueline Griffith

Licence Notes

Front and rear cover design - by Deborah Wood

Printed in the United Kingdom by Printondemand-worldwide.com

A CPI catalogue record for this book is available from the British Library.

ISBN: 978-099346-585-7

The publisher has taken every precaution to ensure that the information contained in this book is accurate and complete.

The legal entity for Ian S Munro is NextStepsGroup Ltd, registered office: 2 Crossways Business Centre, Kingswood, Aylesbury, HP18 0RA, UK

COPYRIGHT OF OTHER AUTHORS:

Books in this series

BLUE BOOKS FOR PERSONAL DEVELOPMENT

100 + TOP TIPS FOR JOB SEEKERS
ISBN 978-095700-853-3

100 + TOP TIPS FOR DEVELOPING YOUR CAREER
ISBN 978-095700-858-8

100 + TOP TIPS FOR EFFECIVE LEADERSHIP
ISBN 978-0-9934658-6-4

100 + TOP TIPS FOR MANAGING YOUR COACHING NEEDS
ISBN 978-0-9934658-7-1

RED BOOKS FOR IMPROVING YOUR ORGANISATION – SMALL AND LARGE

100 + TOP TIPS FOR SETTING UP AND RUNNING AN ONLINE BUSINESS
ISBN 978-099346-580-2

100 + TOP TIPS FOR EFFECTIVE SALES MANAGEMENT
ISBN 978-095700-859-5

100 + TOP TIPS FOR EFFECTIVELY USING ONLINE SOCIAL MEDIA
ISBN 978-099346-582-6

100 + TOP TIPS FOR SETTING UP YOUR OWN BUSINESS
ISBN 978-099346-585-7

100 + TOP TIPS FOR UNDERSTANDING BUSINESS FINANCE
ISBN 978-0-9934658-9-5

Books can be purchased from www.100toptips.com

Introduction

Today we are slap bang in the middle of another Industrial Revolution. How exciting to be here and part of it!

Industrial implies manufacturing and whilst there is still some manufacturing most people today are involved in some part of a "service" industry working environment.

This means you are less likely to be making things – unless you are connected with the engineering industry – more likely to be importing and distributing other manufactured goods or purely selling your knowledge and expertise as a service to individuals or organisations.

Coupled with this "revolution" is a change affecting many people. The change is their desire with others or on their own to set up a business and leave the world of full-time employment

This is one of the most significant trends in the workplace this century!

We meet many people who want to do something new and also be accountable for their own destiny and success.

The common challenge is that most people do not know how to go about this process. It is not complicated. Like anything else in life there are steps to be taken, rules to be complied with and processes which will improve the chances of success.

There are unfortunately failures and many people can fail in their first year. Frankly this is because they did not go about things in a structured planned way nor did they have access to the type of pragmatic hands on advice and tools clearly stated in this book.

Despite the above over the last 20 years we have each been working with people who want to set up their own business and we constantly see people succeeding in all walks of self-employed life.

The 100 + Top Tips series has been written to help individuals and/or organisations by providing snappy bullet point tips which help the reader to develop knowledge, technique and understanding of specific areas in a plain English no nonsense style. Rarely do people have the time to read a great volume, we believe – based on what readers tell us - they need straightforward practical steps to get things moving.

There are two sister books which would also be helpful to you:

100 + TOP TIPS FOR SETTING UP AND RUNNING AN ONLINE BUSINESS ISBN 978-099346-580-2

100 + TOP TIPS FOR UNDERSTANDING BUSINESS FINANCE ISBN 978-0-9934658-9-5

All of our books provide the fundamental steps and tools necessary so that you can take control of your business in the short term and plan your growth and development in the longer term.

For this book you are likely to be one of four types of people;
1. You have a great idea for your business but do not know where to start.
2. You have already set up a business but are not making the progress you expected. How can you improve?
3. A voluntary sector manager who wants to improve the potential for raising funds or even improve operational effectiveness by using the methods and approach outlined in this book.
4. You have recently retired – or are planning retirement – and would like to set up a business a) to keep you interested and active and b) to bring in an additional income stream.

The book covers all the key areas and we plan to have Master Classes through our web site at http://100toptips.com to address specific areas where you would like further information.

A few words about the Learning Zone. Some of the chapters have forms for the reader which are explained in greater depth and illustrated in The Learning Zone. So that the reader can download A4 size blank forms to use on these exercises, go to our book site http://100toptips.com register as a user – your privacy is our priority – and you can download the blank forms.

Hoping you enjoy the book and please let us have any comments at feedback.ownbusiness@100toptips.com

Contents

Getting Started

Getting started is a big decision for everyone thinking of going down this route with ramifications about where you might end up in the next five years and beyond.

We have a useful exercise which allows you to rate yourself on a number of headings and gives you some ideas of what you need to be thinking about.

This exercise is difficult to fit into this book which is neither A5 nor A4.

So we have made the exercise freely available – here is how you can get it!

Firstly visit our website www.100toptips.com and register as a user – we are precious about your data and privacy and pass no information to third parties. Once you have registered you will be able to access the "Learning Zone" and download a .pdf of this exercise.

As a taster, here is what the first page looks like

Enter your mark against each question then total that section. Then read our assessment of your responses.

1 = NOT AT ALL 2 = TO A LIMITED EXTENT 3 = MODERATELY 4 = GREATLY

WORKING ENVIRONMENT For those who are moving from a typical working life there are major changes to be considered. .	1	2	3	4
1 Have you ever worked on your own?				
2 Do you recognise that you might not be part of a team?				
3 Would you like to be on the outside looking in?				
4 Are you prepared to work from home or a small office with reduced contact with others?				
5 Do you have the motivation to get down to work with possible home distractions?				
SECTION TOTAL				
SELF MARKETING In your new role you will be responsible for marketing your services. This is great news as your destiny will be in your hands. How well will you cope?	1	2	3	4
1 Have you ever had to sell yourself or your services?				
2 Would you be able to write a brochure describing your services?				
3 To what extent would you be able to effectively network?				
4 Are you trained/practised/experienced in oral presentations?				
5 Are you trained/practised/experienced in written presentations?				
6 Can you make effective telephone calls to get appointments?				
7 How well would you be capable of handling rejection?				
8 Would you effectively negotiate fees, terms and conditions?				
9 Have you experience of preparing and presenting proposals?				
SECTION TOTAL				

Chapter 1

Top 10 Tips when considering if self-employment is for you

By Jacqueline Griffith

This chapter will help you to decide how well suited you would be to run your own business. Helping you to consider what motivates you, how to tap into your existing work experience and contacts, planning your personal development and your future work/life balance.

1   What motivates you?

- Ego – Are you a naturally positive person with the drive to succeed? Do you have courage and belief in your own abilities? Do you believe you can be successful?
- Money – Are you driven by the desire to make money or just want to generate enough money to pay for your lifestyle?
- Entrepreneurial – Do you want to set up and operate a business taking the risk that it will be successful?
- Freedom – Do you crave creative freedom to design your own products and services? Do you relish autonomy and the ability to make your own commercial decisions?
- Legacy – Do you want to create your own business to pass it on to your children as your legacy for future generations?
- Semi-retirement – Thinking of early retirement but not ready to give it all up yet? Fancy working reduced days?
- Family – Do you have family commitments that dictate the hours you can work, perhaps young children?
- Escape corporate life – Had enough of corporate life and company politics? Prefer to do your own thing?
- Health – A change in health can make you rethink how you spend your working life. Do you need to down shift a little?
- Get a life – Want to find time to improve work / life balance?

2 Do you have any transferrable commercial experience?

- Production – Do you have experience of designing, developing or assembling products?
- Service – Have you worked in the service sector providing services either business to business or business to consumer?
- Operations – This tends to be prevalent in the service sector reflecting the delivery of a service rather than a product.
- Sales – A particularly valuable skill as a self-employed person it is likely you will be selling what you have to offer your customers. Most of us have some shop sales experience from our early work experience.
- Marketing – This is a big bonus if you understand the markets you will be serving, the needs of prospective customers and how to raise awareness of your offering.
- Finance – Fear not you do not need to be a Chartered Accountant, any accounting or bookkeeping experience is valuable even experience of claiming expenses.
- Industry knowledge – If you intend to stay in your previous industry then you have both industry and product knowledge.

3 How good is your network of contacts?

- Never under estimate the power of your network of contacts, they can be a great source of information, advice and contacts.
- Friends – Catch up with old friends that you have embarrassingly lost contact with, yes including lifelong school friends!
- Family – Not just parents and siblings, don't forget uncles, aunts and in-laws particularly if they have any self-employment experience, you never know they may wish to invest in you.

- Neighbours – Not just the people who live near you but local small businesses, preferably non-competitive businesses who may be able to share local market knowledge (see chapter 3 for information on researching competitors).
- Work colleagues – Use LinkedIn.com to find all the people you used to work with but lost track of over the years.
- Customers – Customers from your corporate days, that you previously built a relationship with, could potentially be good customers again so rekindle those relationships.
- Suppliers – Where you have been a valued customer of a supplier in the past it is likely they will welcome you back and potentially give you good terms of business in recognition of your previous trading relationship.
- Professional – Contacts that work in a similar professional function to you will already have a mutual respect for the work you do and can widen the scope of useful contacts in this arena.
- Leisure – Forging relationships with members of your golf club, gym or leisure pursuits can be really useful business contacts.

4   Do you need to be accredited?

- Qualifications – If you are going to be an Electrician or a Heating Engineer you would do well to be qualified before offering your services to your customers. Are you required to be qualified in your area of expertise? If so remember that training and education related to your business will usually be tax deductible.
- Certifications – Will your clients expect you to be certified as proof that you have reached a certain standard of knowledge, for example if you are going to be a Project Manager will they expect you to be Prince 2 Practitioner Certified in project management methodology?

- Training – Certain professions require that you commit to full time training which can include theory and practical work. Bear in mind that sometimes you can work and learn at the same time, for example lecturing and studying for a PGCE simultaneously.
- Apprentice – Sadly not enough companies support Apprenticeships, this is a great way to learn a trade while gaining valuable work experience. Be prepared to volunteer your time if necessary to learn a new skill.
- Assessment – Are you required to undergo ongoing assessment to maintain your professional standard?

5   Do you need professional membership?

- Chartered status – Some people providing their services need the recognition that they have achieved Chartered status and reached a certain professional level for example Chartered Accountants or Chartered Engineers to ensure they are not only a member of an Institute but also qualified to Chartered status.
- Associate membership – You can join many Institutes as an Associate member without being qualified most will look for you to offer some relevant experience instead.
- Student membership – This is often the entry level for membership of an Institute while you are studying for an accredited status.
- Active membership – Be an active member of your professional institute's local group, this where you can build your professional network at little or no cost and pick up some work opportunities!

6   Are you willing to learn?

- Knowledge – Do you need to gain product, industry or market knowledge in areas that are unfamiliar to you? If you are branching out into a new industry, investigate the similarities between your old and new industries, you will be pleasantly surprised at the commercial parallels.
- Skills – Do you need to learn new skills to be able to produce and market your product or service offering? This does not always need to be formal training, if you know people who have the skills you crave can you observe them or offer your time as an unpaid apprentice to gain technical skills. If you need to brush up your IT/Finance/Management skills try your local library they will have free loan books.
- Avoid setting artificial barriers – Don't limit yourself by thinking of the knowledge, skills or experience that you may not have, instead write an action plan of how you will attain them. Adopt a positive attitude and a willingness to learn.

7   Know your personality

If you have previously completed some personality profiling you will already be aware of your attributes. If not consider where you feel your natural tendencies fall within the following:

- Extrovert/Introvert – Do you prefer to externalise or internalise with the world?
- Facts/ Instinct – Do you prefer to work on facts and figures or use your gut feel?
- Head/Heart – Do you make decisions using your head or your heart?

- Structured/Easy going – Are you structured and organised or are you happy to keep your options open and go with the flow?

- Our instincts are often to work with people who are similar to ourselves when in fact you may be more productive if you surround yourself with people who compliment your style.

8 Character traits

There are some character traits that will help if you happen to have any of these then you are ahead of the game:-

- Determination – Having a firm goal in mind and being set on achieving it.
- Resilience – Being adaptable in the face of adversity.
- Self-belief – Confidence in yourself and your abilities.
- Patience – Persevere delays without becoming anxious.
- Vision – Ability to plan the future with imagination.
- Sense of fun – Create a healthy working environment.

9 Lifestyle changes

- You may wish to make some changes to your lifestyle and these can be a trigger to self-employment:
- Hours –You have a young family and would like to spend more time at home. You have decided to improve your work/life balance. You like the idea of working on a contract assignment for a few months and then having a few months off. You have been working 60 hours a week and feel if you are going to put this much effort in then it should be to build your own business not someone else's!

- Location – Perhaps you prefer to work from home or relocate to the country with occasional trips back to the smoke to meet clients.
- Finances – Want to be in control of your finances after your job was affected by redundancy in corporate life? Would you like to work beyond your planned retirement to supplement your pension? Wondering how you can generate an additional income?
- Investment – Do you want to invest in your own business rather than rely solely on investment products?
- Interests – It is possible to take a hobby or interest that you are passionate about and make it your business. This is particularly the case for creative people, a typical example is photography.

10   Stop thinking about it and start today!

- Choose a business structure (see chapter 2 Top 10 tips for choosing a Business Structure.)
- Research your product or service, the market and the demand for your offering (see chapter 3 Top 10 tips for identifying your target market).
- Decide where you will work (see chapter 4 top 10 tips for creating an effective work environment)
- Draft an outline business plan (see chapter 5 Top 10 tips for creating a financial plan and managing risk)
- Consider how you will find customers for your business (see chapter 6 Top 10 tips for winning customers).
- Learn the key aspects of marketing (see chapter 7 Top 10 tips for optimising the marketing mix).
- Design your business operations (see chapter 8 Top 10 tips for product or service operations delivery)
- Decide if you will employ any staff or associates (see chapter 9 Top 10 tips for employing staff or working with Associates)

- Set up your business administration (see chapter 10 Top 10 tips for keeping records, paying taxes and dealing with advisors)

YOUR NOTES FROM CHAPTER 1

Chapter 2

Top 10 Tips for choosing a business structure

By Ian Munro

This chapter brings clarity about the various legal structures and the one you feel meets your needs. Please note that the one you should NEVER consider is as a sole trader. If something goes wrong for whatever reason you could find that your personal assets – house, pension pot, savings etc. - are the only way a disgruntled customer or supplier can realise a claim against you.

1   Understanding the different legal structures

In the UK there are four possible legal structures which you can use for setting up your business. Below we discuss each option and the implications of that option.

- The four options are:
  - Sole Trader
  - Partnership
  - Limited Liability Partnership
  - Limited Liability Company.
- We are in a fortunate situation in the UK that it is relatively inexpensive to set up either option but there are legal and practical implications behind each option which can be read below
- Each option will have an impact on what and when you pay Income Tax and National Insurance
- Visit the **Learning Zone** to find out more.

2   Sole Trader implications

- Becoming a sole trader is the simplest and easiest option.
- You simply give yourself a name and start to offer your service to others. You cannot call yourself a Limited Company if you have not formed one.
- It is a wise step to make sure that you are not copying the name of another existing business, especially one that operates in your geographic area or has a strong web site presence.

- If you are copying a name you could be asked to stop doing so and that means rebuilding your brand or worse being sued by the other party for their loss of income.
- If you are currently employed you will be registered with HMRC (Her Majesty's Revenue and Customs) and paying income tax and National Insurance via PAYE (Pay As You Earn). You need to inform HMRC once you are set up as a sole trader.
- If you are not currently paying via PAYE you need to register as a Self Employed person and arrange to pay your basic National Insurance Contributions.
- You will pay your income tax based initially on your projected income. This will be adjusted once actual figures are known.
- In the UK, you will pay this money to HMRC twice yearly in January and July.
- Many organisations who use sub-contractors or short-term contract staff, do not like using Sole Traders. This is because if you do not pay your tax when due HMRC can go back to your client and blame them for not putting you on a short-term PAYE contract. In many cases HMRC claim the tax back from them.
- You have open ended liability. This means that your personal assets – property, savings, car etc. are at risk of being seized if you are sued by a customer and their claim is successful.
- You can take out insurance to protect against this. This insurance covers legal expenses too, but there are loopholes where a claim can be partly successful – at your expense.
- From a tax perspective, once you deduct expenses from your income the whole balance will be taxable.

- The downside of the Sole Trader is that there is limited relief from either Income Tax or National Insurance contributions.

3   Partnership implications

- The prime difference between sole trader and a partnership is that there are two or more of you.
- All the points mentioned above about registering with HMRC and paying Income Tax and National Insurance apply here.
- All the points about open ended liability equally apply here with a significant difference outlined in the next point.
- The situation though has even greater implications with a Partnership. All the partners have equal and joint liability for the actions and deeds of the other partners.
- This means agreements with customers or suppliers or bankers created by one partner are jointly and severally shared by all the partners.
- As above you can insure against this, however choosing partners means you really need to know with whom you are partnering.
- You do not need to have legal agreements between the parties. You simply say "we have agreed to work together as a partnership."
- We always recommend that you download a partnership agreement from the Internet or a legal advisor.
- The partnership Agreement which can be a simple and straightforward document, states;
  - what the Partnership has been established to do
  - what each partner agrees to do in the partnership
  - Some rules about what you agree not to do are equally important
  - The basis for drawing income from the partnership

- o In the event of a partner being unable to contribute via illness or an accident what happens
- o How the Partnership will be brought to a close or a partner wishes to leave
- We recommend that you seek legal advice from a qualified lawyer.

4   Limited Liability Partnership LLP implications

- The Limited Liability Partnership option was created in 2000 with two main purposes in mind
  - o Provide reduced liability for partners
  - o Provide an international vehicle for organisations operating both within and outside of the UK tax regime
- It is often used in professional bodies – accountants, lawyers
- It provides limited liability to the partners
- For tax purposes it is the members of the partnership who are subject to taxation, not the partnership itself
- The liability of the partners of an LLP is limited to their contribution to the assets of the LLP. Clearly this means it is not open-ended.
- An LLP is registered at Companies House
- There are other issues relating to the structure of the LLP and how it is run. If this is an option for you we suggest you enter "LLP information" into your favourite Search engine – there is lots to read.
- A factor you may wish to consider is based on what a lawyer recently said to me. In the event of a dispute between two Limited Liability Companies we always in the UK refer to Case Law which has been running for hundreds of years. As LLPs were only established in 2000 any cases brought are in effect writing the Case law for LLP.

- The big question for you is if you are entangled with a legal issue as an LLP you could bear the additional expense for lawyer time as there is a limited number of cases to draw upon.
- Out of interest, the earliest recording of Case Law started in the reign of Edward 1 (1239-1307) but in mid Victorian times there was a major campaign to start recording and categorising Case law.

5   Limited Liability Company - implications

- Limited Liability companies as their name implies reduces the liability of the company to the assets in the company's bank account.
- It is the company that is liable not the directors personally. However, there are rules that you have to follow as a director, including acting with a duty of care to the company and its shareholders.
- A Limited Company can be formed;
  o directly on the Companies House website
  o by an accountant
  o by a company that forms the company on your behalf
- There is a step by step guide on the Companies House website and whilst we know how to use the site it should not take longer than 30 minutes to set up the basic information for your business.
- They will then take up to two days to approve your registration request.
- There are two returns that have to be made to Companies House each year
  o A set of the Company Accounts
  o A Confirmation Statement (previously called an Annual Return) listing active directors and their shareholdings
- A limited liability company is a stand-alone legally structured body with its responsibilities and accountabilities.

- You have to keep accurate records of transactions with suppliers and customers. However, this is no different from what you would expect to do in your business.
- For instance, you cannot use a personal bank account for transactions done in the name of the company.
- Setting up a new business account is a simple and straightforward process. At the time of writing the main UK clearing banks will offer free banking from transaction charges for the first two years.
- You would be advised to have public and professional indemnity insurance. These are essential step to take in protecting your business and the assets you will create against the claims of others.
- Public Liability cover insures you against any claims where you may accidentally damage someone else's property or person whilst on their premises. Most people who have contents insurance cover for their home are covered for Public Liability. That cover is for you and your family, not for when you are working under the name of your Limited Company.
- Professional Indemnity Insurance covers you for errors and omissions in your work where a third party has sustained a loss because of what you have or have not done. This cover will exclude acts of negligence on your part – no one can insure for negligence.
- For further information we suggest you enter "Essential Business Insurance" into your favourite search engine.

6   Cost implications of each option…

- **Sole trader** – the costs here are limited as it as simple as setting up and getting on with developing your business.

- The suggested insurances will be covered later in this section. If you appoint an accountant then the estimated costs to do your tax returns will be in the range of £200-300 annually.
- As a sole trader you will pay Income Tax and National Insurance on all of your earnings less expenses.
- Your public liability and professional indemnity costs will be about £250-£300.
- **Partnership** – Our advice here is that you need a written agreement and legal advice to ensure that the Partnership agreement works to the benefit of all partners. This cost based on legal input could be in the range of £500-£1000.
- After expenses the partners will be liable to pay tax on the balance of income.
- Your public liability and professional indemnity costs will be about £250-£300 per partner dependant on the risk level associated with your products and services.
- **Limited Liability Partnership** - As an LLP will be registered at Companies House there will be formation costs of £30 (at time of writing)
- The agreement should be checked by a commercial lawyer which including input for each partner could be around £1,000
- Your public liability and professional indemnity costs will be about £250-£300 per partner dependant on the risk level associated with your products and services.
- After expenses, partners will be liable to pay tax on the balance of income.
- **Limited Liability Compan**y – Based on the option you choose between forming the company yourself, a formations agent or using an accountant the cost will range from £15 to £150
- You should have a Shareholders Agreement which covers issues about day to day activities, who does what, resolving disputes, dissolving the company if necessary.

- An example can be found in the Learning Zone and you would be advised to have a lawyer make sure that Agreement does not contravene the law. Cost estimated at £300-£500.
- Your public liability and professional indemnity costs will be about £300-£400 for the company – as it is the company that is being insured, not the directors - dependant on the risk level associated with your products and services.
- The tax situation with Limited Companies is different from the other options as follows
    - After the deduction of expenses, the balance will be subject to Corporation Tax currently around 19%
    - Retained profit in the company is not taxed
    - A basic salary to the directors will be taxed normally
    - Dividends paid to directors will be subject to Dividend Tax of 7.5% rising to 38.1% based on your tax band. Currently there is a tax free dividend allowance of £2,000.

7   What are the risks you will be facing.

- It would be advisable to do a risk analysis for your business to make sure
    - firstly, that you are aware of the potential risks
    - secondly, have an outline plan covering what you will do if any risk becomes a reality...
- We consider that any business – whether a one-man band or a multinational venture has three key functional drivers listed here not in order of importance
    - Sales and marketing
    - Operations to include manufacturing and delivery of services and/or products fulfilment
    - Finance and legal
- If any one of the three malfunctions then the business is at risk

- Any large business is likely to have Human Resources, Information Technology as other functions but the three listed above are mission critical
- When you compile your Risk Analysis you need to separate the risks into High Medium and Low
- A number of Risk Analysis formats can be found by entering "Risk Analysis" in your favourite search engine.

8   Will you be subcontracting work to others

- Sub-contracting features in many businesses today. For example, consultants subcontract to other consultants. Builders sub contract to tradesmen.
- This is an ideal way to add resources to your business without having to employ staff with all the related costs.
- However there a number of pitfalls which you need to be aware of.
- Part of your development plans should be to identify possible resources so that if you have a sudden increase in business you can meet this new demand promptly
- From a legal perspective, you should make sure that your sub-contractor is bound by the same terms and conditions to you that you have with your customer.
- They should also have their own public liability and indemnity insurance. If they cause a customer claim, the customer will claim against you. You need to be in a position to counter claim against the sub-contractor.

9   Will you be manufacturing and distributing goods?

- This Chapter is mainly about legal structures and in these structures you need to have an understanding about what you need to do to protect your business.

- Once you start either manufacturing – even home based – and/or distributing goods you really have to recognise the potential risks for liability so please either have a limited company or an LLP.

10   Helping you to make a decision

- We recommend that you read our Decision Making Process in the Learning Zone item 4
- This should bring clarity about the best ways to proceed
- It is also a useful guide because sometimes we let our heart rule our mind and using this tool helps us to see the more obvious step.
- It can be helpful to identify a mentor with whom you can share your ideas. This could be someone you have worked with or a close friend.
- Sometimes those not really close to us can bring a less passionate opinion about our plans and goals!

YOUR NOTES FROM CHAPTER 2

Chapter 3

Top 10 Tips for identifying your target market

By Jacqueline Griffith

This chapter will encourage you to decide on your chosen target market for your business. How to profile and target your typical customers. How to differentiate what you have to offer to maximise revenue potential. It also covers the value of market research.

1   Are you selling to organisations or consumers?

- Will your customers be organisations within the private or public sectors? In other words are you selling Business to Business (B2B)?
- Will your customers be individual consumers are you therefore selling Business to Consumer (B2C)?

2   What is the profile of your target customer?

- Profiling your typical customers will enable you to target your products or services to groups of similar customers.
- In which industry sector will your B2B customers be operating? Are they manufacturing a product or providing a service?
- What is the typical size of the organisation you are targeting? What is their annual sales revenue or how many employees do they have?
- If you are targeting consumers, what are the demographic variables of your target consumer? Consider their lifestyle, income bracket, gender, age, type and location of the property they live in. What other characteristics typify your customers?

3   Have you segmented your market?

- Having profiled your customers you probably determined that they fall into natural segments because customers are not usually homogenous.
- Find out why your customers want to buy your product or service.

- Different people may have different motives for buying the same product for example some want a car with a boot big enough to accommodate a set of golf clubs, others a pram.
- Is there variation in consumption amongst your target group of customers? If so, you may wish to have a strategy for attracting high users.
- How will you encourage customer loyalty? Some customers may be fiercely loyal to their existing provider others may switch at the first sign of a perceived benefit from another supplier. Consider strategies for attracting and retaining both groups.
- Consider regional and cultural customer differences.
- What type of buying organisation are you dealing with? Do industrial organisations buy through a centralised head office function or allow subsidiaries to make their own buying decisions? This will affect the policies of marketing to these organisations.
- Review all the potential segments you could serve and assess the profitability of each before deciding on which segments to target.
- Produce products and services that will appeal to the chosen segments of your market to maximise their appeal.

4   What are your geographical boundaries?

- The world is your oyster what geographical boundaries do you intend to impose on your business?
- You may be setting up your business to serve the local community will no intentions of expanding but you may gain a great reputation which spreads on the internet and by social media and before you know it you are exporting word-wide. So best to consider your chosen geographical boundaries for sales and delivery of your product or service from the outset.

- Will your business be local, regional, national or international? You could decide to start the business on a regional basis with the intention of expanding the area in future years.

5 Know customers' typical buying triggers.

- What are the buying patterns of your customers? Are they likely to have the luxury of planned procurement or a panic buy? If you are selling toner cartridges some of your customers will keep a stock in reserve while others will run out before they order a replacement.
- What are the buying requirements of your customers' business? Customers can make apparently unreasonable demands but once you understand their needs you will appreciate why they have made those demands. For example, they want you to deliver out of hours because they have made delivery promises to their customers.
- What will motivate your customers to order from you? Quality, service, price or a specific combination of these? Ask your customers what their buying criteria are for selecting their suppliers. See **Learning Zone Item 3** Customer requirement Analysis

6 Will your customers buy multiple offerings?

- It is easy to sell one product or service to a customer and forget to cross-sell your other offerings. Always look out for opportunities to identify alternative customer requirements that you may be able to satisfy.
- Is there potential to sell complimentary services?

- For example if you are selling lawn mowers you could also offer a maintenance service and perhaps the added value of an optional collection and delivery service.

7   What are your competitors offering?

- Identify your market competitors. What are they offering, what are their terms and conditions and what is their pricing policy?
- You can do a huge amount of desk research on the internet. For example, if you are a plumber offering a trade service there are websites who check the validity of registered traders and offer customers the chance to visibly review the service they received.
- Prior to setting up your business you could invite competitors to provide you with a quotation. A great way to gain valuable insight into how they operate.
- If you have already set up your business then ask your personal contacts to obtain competitor information for you.
- Form working relationships with close competitors on the understanding that if you are too busy to accommodate a customer request you could recommend that competitor. This is a common practice with hotels when they have full occupancy.

8   What is your Unique Selling Point?

- What is different about your business and what you have to offer? Customers need to be able to differentiate you from your competitors.
- You can find many ways of making your offering more compelling. For example, if you are offering energy efficiency consulting, is there a minimum potential saving that the customer could enjoy if they followed all your recommendations?

- If you are a food hygiene trainer and your past customers have improved their Food Hygiene scores for their restaurants that could make you a very attractive proposition.
- Businesses are trying to promote the perception of a better service e.g. same day delivery, extended warranties, dedicated account manager. What are you offering that makes you stand out?
- Spend time on this and it will repay you handsomely.

9   Do your market research.

- We have already looked at your competitor research but there is much more to research.
- How big is your potential market?
- What are the characteristics of the segments you intend to target?
- What are the trends in your chosen market? What is on the up?
- Research your potential customers and their buying habits.
- What other products are available that are similar to yours?
- Check the price point that would be acceptable to your prospective customers for your offering.
- Evaluate the viability of the marketing communications methods open to you including digital marketing, advertising, sales promotion and public relations activity.
- Published market data is available at a price from research report publishers but look out for free statistical information published by government agencies and trade associations and don't forget the Business Directories in your local library!
- So far we have looked at mostly desk research but you can also test the customer acceptability of your product. You can set up focus groups, present your business idea and ask if they would buy your product or service and at what price.

- Create a questionnaire and survey prospective customers to gain greater customer insight.
- Arrange market research meetings with prospective B2B customers to understand their business requirements and how your business should be operated to support the needs of that customer type.
- Talk to suppliers they can be a valuable source of information.
- Are there physical location issues for your business that may influence your proximity to your key markets? There are concentrations of certain industries in different parts of the UK, do you need to be near to any of them?

10   Be prepared to be demand led.

- You may have a clear idea of the service you wish to provide but your clients may have other ideas. For example, a Garden Designer may find that the customer expects them to not only produce a plan of which plants to plant and where but wishes them to purchase the plants and plant them too!
- Watch out for changing customer needs and how you can satisfy those needs profitably.
- Be ahead of the market in embracing technology to improve your efficiency. There are very affordable data management and communications equipment that can give you an edge in your market and be ahead of the change curve.

YOUR NOTES FROM CHAPTER 3

Chapter 4

Top 10 Tips for creating an effective working environment

By Ian Munro

So you believe you have a great business idea and you start to get interest in your venture. If you and others are going to work from someone's back room at home, that doesn't always create an effective environment. Sometimes the demand can take off quickly, so unless you have done some pre-planning – read this chapter for a start - you can suddenly find that the business is driving you rather then you driving this business.

1   Premises - home

- It is a very attractive option for people to start a business from home. There are no landlord or business rates to pay.
- You need to check that there is not a constraint with your mortgage provider – if you have one – that prevents you from running a business from home.
- In most cases this is not an issue if you are simply operating without a need for warehousing and stock holding. Basically, it is you and one or two others running a desk/PC based business.
- If you are having people operating out of your home you will still need separate insurance for employee and public liability. There might be other local constraints from running a business from home.
- You will also have to comply with Health and Safety at work regulations and fire regulations relating to access and exit issues.

2   Premises – rent/buy
- If the needs of the business show that you need to operate from premises, then you have a buy or rent/lease options. We would never recommend that premises were purchased until there is strong evidence that your business model really works and a longer-term property purchase becomes a viable option.

- Even then until you have been through at least one 12-month business cycle you need to fully evaluate whether funds should be used for property purchase or kept as working capital as the business grows.
- In the UK there are Local Government initiatives to provide low cost rental units – offices and warehouses – for start-up businesses. These are often rented rather than leased which provides greater flexibility for you the tenant.
- A quick word about renting versus leasing. Renting is all very straightforward where you have an agreement to rent premises for a period of time with fair notice of termination between the parties. The basic version of this is called a licence and is a very flexible way of renting. Leasing is a more complex arrangement with a fixed period for the lease often 3, 5, 10 years or more. There can be tough penalties to be paid if you try to end the lease earlier than the agreed date.

3 IT issues

- We have split this into four main areas
- Hardware
  - o There is a common risk when people setting up a business overly specify their equipment needs. In the early days cash is critical so do not be tempted to buy the most expensive equipment just because you believe you can.
  - o We recommend the use of laptops because they are portable, they are also more secure. If you are working from an office you can continue to do so from home if you have the laptop with you.
  - o If you are travelling your office goes with you!
- Software
  - o Specify what are the IT needs likely to be in the first year.

- o If you are personally providing a service based on your expertise and track record you need nothing other than an up to date "office suite". This can be sourced from Microsoft but "Open Office" which can be freely downloaded from Oracle is a very effective suite just like Microsoft Office.
  - o If you have a high volume of customers because you have a business which is distributing goods then you need to consider a CRM (Customer Relationship Management) system which includes customer details, their ordering and delivery record and includes also the record of their invoices and payments.
  - o Most of these systems come in a modular form where you have a starter system that has add-ons as your business grows.
- Development needs in a growing business.
  - o Based on early demand patterns you should be considering your future needs.
  - o Adding software changes is not like just bolting on another piece like building with Lego.
  - o There will be costs involved so you need to work closely with your software provider to ensure that your system grows in line with business growth and affordability.
- Security
  - o We have all read of the horror stories that some businesses incur through hacking, theft of business identity and financial loss through phishing.
  - o Do not take shortcuts here by skimping on appropriate security systems to reduce your risk of attack
  - o Don't be blinded by the old habits of taking a daily back up of your transactions.
  - o Make sure that all your records are backed up – probably through a "cloud" based system – in real time.

- The villains who are likely to attack can do so at any time. They operate globally and around the clock.

4   Equipment

- Making product
    - If you are involved in manufacturing, what is the best and most cost-effective way to source essential equipment?
    - Do you buy new or second hand?
    - Do you buy at all, or do you lease?
    - How do you source raw materials?
    - Do you buy from local wholesalers/suppliers or do you source internationally with obvious investment issues from raw material stockholding?
- Packing
    - How will your product be packaged and what about outer packaging?
    - Will you use a package designer to reduce the impact on your costs of shipping air through bad packaging design?
- Shipping
    - Shipping – including postal costs often split into three categories; UK, European (EU) and Rest of World (ROW). Some businesses appoint a distributor in each country, ship to them in bulk and they handle deliveries on a local basis.
    - Apart from reducing costs this also improves security because in country to in country postage is often more secure than postal from another country.
- Returns
    - There are a host of reasons why returns are made so do not assume they will not happen.
    - Just as you will have a secure process for recording orders despatched it is equally important to log returns and relate them to the original order.

- o A good CRM system should incorporate a returns process.

5 Customer journey/experience

- Initially you should create on a spreadsheet the various points of your customer's journey. This should include customers buying your expertise as well as those buying goods. An example can be seen in the **Learning Zone**
- ...Each journey will have a waypoint where an activity happens. This can be seen in the examples but could be when a quotation for a service is made, followed by a follow up point or date, followed by receipt of an order, followed by an acknowledgment and so on.
- Any complaints or customer queries can be logged against the waypoint where the problem occurred. A pattern should emerge about the weak points in your customer journey which gives you control over what you should be doing to correct that issue.
- Customers should be encouraged to give feedback – through your website – about their experience – good and bad.
- Resolving issues relating to the customer journey will have a significant effect on improving your working environment.

6 Time Management

- Distractions –
  - o Because initially there is likely to be a few of you running the business it will be easy to be distracted and focus on issues of the day rather than what you had pre planned to be that day's activity.
  - o For instance you may have planned to work on next month's sales promotion but instead you take the day up with resolving customer service issues.

- o Dealing with customer issues is clearly important. However by acknowledging the issue with the customer/s and agreeing to get back to them in 24 hours allows you to focus on your original plan.
    - o As the business grows developing a culture where time is not wasted because of poor planning and implementation will be critical to your success.
- Cost impact –
    - o An inefficient process will impact on time and time is money
    - o By setting yourself a sensible daily workload you will achieve results across a range of tasks.

7   Communications

The aim of good communications is to provide a free flow of information up and down your business and across departments or functions. We work in many businesses from the very small to the very big. The root cause of many of the problems we address is based in poor communications.

In broad terms communication affects the following

- Suppliers
    - o Suppliers play a key part because without suppliers you cannot provide customers with the appropriate goods or services
    - o Supplier communications include updated forecasts of your needs in terms of volume and timing
- ...Customers
    - o As mentioned above your CRM system should cover off essential customer communications

- Internal
  - Apart from outside customers as your business grows different internal departments have internal customers who are relying on each other for information and communications. You will need to create clear communication channels across your venture.
- External
  - External is obviously suppliers but also your business is likely to have professional advisers – accountants, legal, advisors who need to be kept informed about progress so that they can help to get things back on track if needed. Also communicating through social media – including your web site – is a very positive way of letting others know about events and developments in your venture.

8   Customer Management Criteria

- Basic principles
  - We have outlined above the need for CRM systems which are designed to deal with the process.
  - You also need to agree standards and time scales for each stage of the customer journey and for responding to customer enquiries, queries and complaints.
  - It is likely to be you initially but as the venture grows you will need to delegate some and eventually all of this responsibility to someone else.
- Training and monitoring
  - Applying the criteria applies to everyone. Your venture needs to create a strong customer focussed ethos and culture right from the beginning. This means that all new starters need to be trained in your beliefs and processes.

- Also remember that ongoing monitoring will ensure that your standards are not slipping due to the pressures of a growing business.
- Feedback
  - Encourage customer feedback. Understanding the good and bad is important in terms of how you structure a growing business.
  - One of the things I like about "Trip Advisor" is under Customer reviews for a venue there is also the opportunity for the venue to respond to a negative feedback.
  - On your web site you can encourage customers to give their feedback to which you can respond – to the good as well as the bad.

9   Networking and contacts

- Not being isolated
  - Part of the challenge in a new business can be loneliness. Initially you may be on your own and over even a short period of time this can impact on your working environment.
  - When you start bringing others into the business they too may have been used to a larger organisation and might find working in a small group challenging.
  - Be aware of this and look after these people. As an example some businesses we have worked with will take the team out for a pizza (or a team walk or even a run) every Tuesday lunch time. They get a break and it's good to grow a team feeling in what is a fairly inexpensive way
- Become involved at local/regional level
  - In your town or city there may be a trade association for small businesses which allows you to hear how others are getting on and these organisations also provide a support mechanism for ventures just like yours.

- o Sometimes there may be regional groupings which could be focused on your trade/business area. Getting a voice in such an organisation will also play a part in developing the wider awareness of you and your businesses and may well play a part in developing new business.
- Networking on a broader basis
  - o We are absolute fans of networking either on a face to face basis or via social networking sites such as LinkedIn.
  - o On a face to face basis we are not so keen on large networking events with lots of people milling around attempting to get their message across, In the Learning Zone is an extract from a sister book about "Becoming a great networker"

10   Reviewing, updating and developing

- Creating a positive work environment for you and colleagues will pay dividends as the business grows.
- You will need to formally review Marketing, Operations and Financial issues on a regular basis – we suggest monthly.
- Even though you are "pushed" for time make sure you keep these reviews running.
- We recommend that working environment covers all of the above 3 but probably relates more to the Operations area.
- Make sure that "working environment" remains on your monthly review agenda!

YOUR NOTES FROM CHAPTER 4

Chapter 5

Top 10 Tips for creating a financial plan and managing risk

By Jacqueline Griffith

The following is to give you an understanding of the basics. We would always recommend that you seek advice and guidance from a small business accountant. Remember to look at our sister book 100 + Top Tips for understanding Business Finance

1   Will you make a Profit or a Loss?
- We have already mentioned the importance of profit. Clearly your business will not be sustainable in the medium to long term if it is unable to generate a profit surplus. This is your time, effort and money so it is worth running the numbers early to check that the revenue you will generate less the operational costs will deliver a profit. (Refer to the P & L template in the Learning Zone.)
- Sales budget – Build up your planned revenue from the anticipated spend per customer, plotting it in the month you expect to invoice your customer, bear in mind this will probably be on delivery of your goods or services.
- Cost of Sales budget – List the direct costs associated with producing your product particularly materials and direct labour.
- Gross Profit – is sales revenue less direct costs.
- Overheads – Now consider all the other expenses associated with running a business including: salaries, premises, travel / transport, insurance and interest; plot them in the month you will be invoiced by your suppliers. Overheads in a service business may well represent most or all of the costs.
- Net Operating Profit – is Gross Profit less overheads.
- Cyclical implications – Will your business have notably busy and quiet months throughout the year? If you are selling Christmas trees you will probably sell most of your stock in December.

- Offering garden landscaping could be a good supplementary source of revenue for other parts of the year. On the other hand there are consultants who only work 6 months of the year in the UK and spend the other 6 months in their Mediterranean villas!
- Three-year Profit & Loss projection – Most businesses only look one year ahead but it is worth planning how your business will grow over the next 3 years and the associated investment that you will need.
- Review your budgeted profit and loss against the actual figures, analyse the variances and do not be afraid to make changes to the plan if needed.

2   Will you have enough cash in the bank?

- Cash is King!
- Many businesses fail through a lack of cash flow rather than profitability. Complete a monthly cash flow forecast to plot all your revenue and expense lines for the business at the date you anticipate they will be credited or debited to your bank account (see the template for this in the Learning Zone).
- The liquidity of a business is the measure of the working capital or cash available. You need to monitor your cash in bank position to avoid running out of cash to then find yourself unable to pay your creditors.
- Worst case scenario is that you lose all the money you invested in the business or could find yourself a declared bankrupt so watching the cash flow is key.
- Trading whilst insolvent is an offence so ensure your business is solvent by having sufficient assets (cash, stock and debtors) to cover your liabilities (loans and creditors).

- If you are in the enviable position of having large amounts of cash in your business do not leave it all in your current account, ask your bank about deposit arrangements that will generate some interest.

3   Will you need to invest in capital equipment?

- If you need equipment to be able to create and promote your product or service then you may need to invest significant sums of money in buying that equipment either new or used. Examples are production machinery, tools, IT office equipment (including a laptop and printer), telephones and furniture for your business premises. These are your business assets.
- Plan all the assets you will need and take advantage of the annual capital investment allowance available to businesses through HMRC which you can offset against your profits and potentially reduce your tax liability.
- Set up an Asset Register to log all your business assets and their current value.
- Depreciation is an annual allowance for wear and tear on equipment. Assets have a predicted whole life, for example vehicles may be 5 years or IT equipment may be 3 years. Take a laptop that cost £900, each year you would deduct £300 for depreciation against your costs.
- You would normally depreciate the value of an asset over the expected life of the asset to spread the cost of purchase in your accounts; this cost is allowable as a business expense. Take advantage of any government annual investment allowance to offset the cost of purchasing equipment in the year of purchase rather than depreciating it over several years.

- Do you really need to own all your assets? If you need a very expensive piece of equipment for occasional use it may be more cost effective to rent that equipment and avoid the need to insure, store and maintain it.
- Leasing
  - o A finance lease is a type of equipment lease where the customer (or 'lessee') rents an asset for most of the item's useful life. Finance leases are sometimes also known as capital leases.
  - o One key feature of finance leases is that the customer takes on most of the risks and rewards of ownership (i.e. maintenance costs and fluctuations in value), but never actually owns the asset.
  - o What this means in practice is that a finance lease looks and feels a lot like hire purchase, but they're different on the balance sheet.
  - o Finance leases consist of a primary rental period, where the monthly payments will add up to the full cost of the asset plus interest (hence their other name, *capital* leases).
  - o Once the primary period is up, the asset will normally be near the end of its useful life. At the end of the primary lease period, you will usually have three options:
  - o Continue to use the asset in a secondary lease period (often with cheaper payments)
  - o Sell the asset and keep a share of income from the sale
  - o Return the asset to the lessor

4   How will you fund your working capital?

- Aside from the equipment you will need there will be running expenses to keep your business afloat.

- Typically these include business rent, rates, staff costs, raw materials, bank charges, communications and promotional costs. Do you have enough cash in your business bank account to cover any negative cash flow months? How will you pay these bills if there is insufficient cash flow at any point in time? You will need cash reserves.
- If you are going to use a bank overdraft make sure you have a pre-agreed business overdraft limit with reasonable fees; exceeding your agreed overdraft limit can be expensive in interest rates and fees so should be avoided!
- Banks like secured lending so if you are going to borrow money you will normally enjoy better rates by securing a loan against an asset. For example, if you borrow money to buy a car the bank will secure the load against the car in case you default on the repayments but be aware that if you do not keep up the payments you will lose your asset!
- Collect the money you are owed by your debtors within the agreed credit limit and timescales. A customer who does not pay you is not a customer but a liability!
- Negotiate the most generous credit terms you can achieve without incurring interest penalties from your suppliers.
- Keep a tight rein on your stock levels, that includes raw materials, work in progress and finished product (service businesses can also use materials).
- Ordering materials in vast quantities can be tempting if you qualify for higher discounts but this requires a commensurate commitment of spend for materials that may take months or years to consume.
- Many large businesses work on low stock levels by convincing their suppliers to hold stock available on a just-in-time delivery basis. This may not be an option for small quantities but you would be surprised at the terms you can achieve by asking.

5   What happens when you need emergency funding?

- Personal savings – Do you have savings that you can draw on that are in easy access accounts, or will there be an interest penalty if you make withdrawals?
- Directors' loans – If you are a director of a Limited company then as a director you can make a director's loan to your company which the company will need to repay and therefore the loan will become a liability to the business. Repaying that loan in part or full will not incur a tax liability to you.
- Family member loans – Do you have family members who are cash rich and willing to lend you some money should you need it? Parents have been known to advance some inheritance as a gift.
- Overdrafts – As previously mentioned interest on overdrafts can be expensive particularly if you exceed your overdraft limit so consider your overdraft facility requirements carefully rather than relying on the nominal sum recommended by the bank when you set up your business account.

6   How will you distribute the shares in your business?

- How many directors will you appoint to the business? Will they all be entitled to own some ordinary shares? This will dictate their ability to draw a dividend, vote at meetings and be entitled to capital should the company close.
- The company can also issue 'preference shares', which have a fixed right to dividends and no voting rights.
- Although you may be primarily concerned with share dividend distribution initially, do not overlook the power of voting rights.

- I know someone who set up a business with his life partner with a share capital split of 50/50 in hindsight they wished they had set it up 49/51 so the originator had a controlling share.
- Commonly in small businesses 100 shares are issued. If you are unsure how many shares to issue to maintain a simple structure for your business, obtain some professional advice from your accountant.

7   Costing and Pricing

- There are many ways to price your product or service. Clearly the price charged must cover production costs, overheads and produce a profit.
- The ideal game plan is to minimise cost and maximise price. Selling at the most the market will pay to maximise profit.
- Some businesses use a cost plus basis. For example a builder may cost the materials and labour required for a build and add a percentage for his profit to calculate the price he will charge.
- If you are providing a service and the main cost is the provision of your time then you can calculate your cost per hour by assessing the annual overheads plus your own anticipated drawings from the business divided by the total number of productive hours per annum. Bear in mind that you will probably only work a maximum of 47 weeks per annum allowing for holidays and sickness and that productive hours per week will be reduced by time spent on sales and administration.
- If you are manufacturing a product then the calculation of the cost per unit is similar using overheads divided by the total number of units, then add the production cost per unit. If you have multiple products then you will need to apportion production costs and overheads to each product.

- Now you have the costs calculated you can add a profit margin and VAT, if you are VAT registered, to produce a price.
- If you are selling business to business prices excluding VAT are normally quoted and your terms clearly say "prices exclude VAT".
- If you are selling business to consumer prices are shown including VAT with the statement "prices include VAT"
- Market forces must also be taken into account when setting prices and this is covered in Chapter 7 "Optimising the Marketing Mix".

8   Have you conducted a risk assessment?

- What percentage of your personal wealth do you intend to invest in your business? If the business fails will you still own sufficient personal wealth?
- Will you employ staff? If so you have a duty of care for those people while they are working. What are the risks of injury to them while in your employ?
- If you are providing consultancy advice and your clients suffer a financial loss as a result of implementing your advice how much could your client sue you for?
- If you are providing a product and your product causes personal injury, how much could your customer sue you for?
- Do you have customers visiting your premises, if so if they are injured during their visit how much could they potentially sue you for?
- Are you working on your customers' premises, if someone trips over your equipment on site and injures themselves they may claim for damages?
- Are you carrying out work to your customers' property that could cause damage? For example a tree surgeon felling a tree near a very expensive house could risk a high claim for damages.
- Do you rely on the specialist knowledge of a key member of your team? Can you replace that knowledge?

- Are your business premises in a flood plain? If so what is the probability that you will be flooded?
- Have you created a unique product or concept, if so can it be freely copied or have you patented it?
- Do you need to protect your intellectual property if so consider registering a trade mark.
- How secure is your computer system? Do you have adequate firewall and antivirus protection? Do you regularly back up your data? Are your PCs in a vulnerable physical location?
- Do you need to store valuable tools or equipment on your premises? How vulnerable is that equipment and how can you protect it?
- Do you have a specially adapted vehicle for your business and if so how will you find a substitute if the vehicle is off the road?

9   Do you have adequate insurance cover?

- Having conducted your risk assessment you may wish to mitigate some of these risks with some insurance cover. Insurance premiums will add to your costs but if you decide to self-insure these risks then treat them as a potential liability.
- We have listed some of the insurances available but be aware that you may need other insurances depending on the nature of your business.
- Employers' liability – As an employer you have a duty of care to your employees and so if you are going to employ staff then you should ensure you have adequate Employers Liability insurance in the event that your employees are injured in the course of their work, typically at least £5m sum insured, with high fines for non-compliance. There are exceptions to complying with this requirement if you only employ immediate members of your family (this exemption does not apply to family businesses incorporated as limited companies)

- Also if you employ people abroad, however, you should check whether the law in the country where they are based requires you to take out insurance.
- Buildings: Commercial and home – If you intend to use commercial premises it would be prudent to insure the buildings and contents (including any tools and equipment). If you are using your home in a way that alters your home from solely domestic use then you should inform your home insurer. For example if you are manufacturing pots in your garage you may require planning consent for change of use and your insurer will wish to apply commercial risk cover to this area of the property. If you are storing high value tools on your property you would do well to declare this fact to your insurer in case they are stolen and not covered under your home insurance.
- Equipment – Ensure plant, machinery and tools are covered particularly if you are a trade's person and you rely on the stock of tools you have built up over the years. Ensure they are covered where you store them and on customer sites.
- It is also worth checking if they are covered when in vehicles as this can often be a policy exclusion.
- Car – Remember to add "business use" to your car insurance if you intend to use your own car other than to commute to one place of work.
- Commercial vehicles - insurance should cover the vehicle chassis and bodywork.
- Goods-in-transit - insurance to cover the vehicle load. Insurers vary their premiums according to the value and perishability of the load. High value and temperature controlled goods may attract higher premiums.

- Compensation is often calculated on a cost per tonne basis so if you have high value goods to cover ensure you are not penalised by a pre-set low value per tonne.
- Professional Indemnity – If as a consultant your customer suffers financial loss as a result of your recommendations they may sue you. Depending on their business and their potential losses this could be in the millions. Premiums vary considerably for this cover but if you are a member of a professional institute or trade association you may be able to gain this cover at a modest fee.
- Public liability – In the event that customers or a member of the public suffers personal injury caused by an event on your premises you are liable. It is likely you will have public liability included in your home insurance but if you have customers visiting your home and you have not advised your insurer you will probably find this will be excluded.
- Product liability - If you sell a product and the buyer suffers damage or personal injury from the use of your product they may sue you so do ensure you have adequate insurance to cover you for the worst that could happen.
- It is also a good idea to ensure safety precautions are adequately displayed in any product instruction leaflet.
- Business interruption – If you have business premises affected by flooding the buildings insurance will cover the repairs to the fabric of the building but not the loss of revenue because you cannot open your doors to your customers, so consider if you need cover for loss of revenue because you cannot trade.

- Personal accident & sickness/critical illness – If you have an accident and suffer personal injury or become sick and cannot work these policies can provide a replacement income but be aware these policies can include many exclusions so check the small print!
- Private medical – Remaining healthy and fit for work is a must if you are self-employed as you will probably have little in the way of sick pay and the PMI cover you had in corporate life will have ended so you need to decide if this is something you want to continue enjoying. These insurers tend to exclude pre-existing conditions so if you have a medical condition that you need continuous cover for then it may be worth obtaining a quote from your previous employer's insurer.
- Finally our advice is to seek an insurance review from a qualified insurance broker who is registered to give advice by The Financial Conduct Authority. On the basis that you will be placing business with them the review should be fee free.

10   Have you drafted a disaster plan?

- If you are fearful of how you will cope if disaster befalls your business, use that energy to list everything that could go wrong and then create a contingency plan to deal with those issues.
- If you are ill who will do the work? If you are a sole trader buddy up with some trusted associates that are willing to work with you. They can invoice you for their time and you can retain the relationship with your customer.
- If your premises become unusable where will you transfer your operation to temporarily to maintain business continuity?

- If your car is in an accident do you have access to an alternative vehicle? Or do you know the local public transport infrastructure? Don't wait for disaster to strike and then worry how you are going to deal with it, plan ahead.

YOUR NOTES FROM CHAPTER 5

Chapter 6

Top 10 Tips for winning customers

By Ian Munro

This chapter is all about the important steps you need to take to develop a process that helps you to win customers. This is NOT about pure selling, but the infrastructure that you will need to put in place to 1) give great customer service and 2) ensure your good work is known to many people.

1   Identifying and confirming needs

- Are you really sure you know what they want? First step in winning customers is not your sales pitch. It is the time investment you make to look at the market and current trends.
- It's not about what you want to sell. When we advise people setting up a business there is a tendency for them to want to sell what they think customers need. Try not to get too focused on what you think they need.
- Has your research identified customer needs? A good place to validate your findings is to talk to friends and your network about whether they believe the market is where you think it is.

2   Creating a positive customer journey

- Have you created the journey on paper or on a spreadsheet? Most of us will have a vision in our minds about how things will work. Those working with us may have a different view point. You must have a clear vision. Mapping out the customer journey on a piece of paper is a good start. However using a spreadsheet makes it easier to change and you can save different versions to keep a record of where changes have been made.
- Have you tested the timing from beginning to end? It might seem a usage of time that you cannot afford when you are busy setting up. It is a necessary investment though if you are supplying a product. Include in the test despatching product to see how long this part of the journey takes.

- What are the potential log jams? The testing will show up the log jams. They may not just be in the distribution area. There could be delays in the paying procedure, or your own mail system.
- How will you get feedback? Listen to all the feedback from those helping at the testing stage. Sometimes we don't want to hear the bad news that something has gone wrong. Listen to and action all input. Next time it might be a customer who becomes an ex customer because their journey was not a success.

3 Fast response to queries

- How will the queries come in? We have discussed before setting up a CRM system to monitor queries. You need to create for all customers a "fast track" method for dealing with their queries.
- Who will be responsible for monitoring and response? Rather than it just being you all the time establish a rota to share the workload of monitoring and dealing with queries. Make sure your system lists who dealt with the query, when the customer was contacted and any response from them.
- Remember the potential damage via social media. Some customers today respond via social media to show their displeasure that something has gone wrong. The smart suppliers like you respond quickly expressing their regret that something went wrong and also saying what they did to rectify that situation.

4 Create a simple web presence
- Successful web sites demonstrate that "less is more" Whilst you feel "proud" about constructing a complex web site with many subpages, are you meeting customer needs with this approach?
- Easily navigated sites bring clarity about your product and/or services.

- Update content regularly. Apart from improving your search engine visibility, you need to show that you are up to date with your offering and are following the latest trends. The customer will see this and accept that they are buying from an up to date organisation
- Encourage and incentivise visitor feedback. Show through the web site that you value customer feedback even at the customer journey phase. List customer comments good and bad with your response. Do not identify the customer by location as you could be infringing customer data protection information. On the incentive front you can give a discount voucher – 5, 10 or 15% off next order in exchange for feedback.

5   Be highly visible on Social media

- Encourage two way traffic. This is becoming a common theme in this chapter as we encourage you to have open and regular communication. It is a key part of the customer journey.
- Keep abreast of new developments. By giving your opinion on social media about trends and developments it is letting your prospective customer see that you are a voice in your sector.
- Be very customer centric. Make sure you are communicating your strong focus on customer service. Tell them again and again about your prime focus on customer service.

6   Monitor enquiries, conversion rates

- Compare results with previous days, weeks and months. Identify if there are patterns which are day and/or time related. Does new business tend to happen on certain days and times?
- Will increasing volumes on these days and times mean that the customer journey is likely to be delayed or affected in some other way?

- Examine slow down or lower conversion rates. Why are there changes to the pattern of orders? Is it to do with events like pay days and or holiday periods?
- Keep a close eye on the competition. Some larger competitors will have more resources than you in the early days to check out trends and the need for change. Visit their websites regularly and read any blogs that may give you a clue that some changes are on the way which you too may have to consider.

7   Networking visibility

- Never forget the power of the network. Arguably networking is more relevant if you are selling a service. I would disagree with this because a well thought out social media campaign can create a form of networking where regular users are part of "your club" They are a really valuable source of information and referrals see next paragraph.
- It is physical as well as on line. Within your local community and in any trade sector bodies you will have the chance to meet, network and communicate what you are doing. Offer to be a speaker at events. This will help you to be seen as a subject expert in your field of business.
- Face to face individually is 100 times more effective than events. Events are useful for identifying those with whom you would like to have a face to face discussion. The **Learning Zone** has a section on "Becoming a great networker".

8   Create a referrals platform
- Win customers because of what others say. In the travel business Trip Advisor has become a great source for customer feedback.
- Other trade organisations have developed in a similar way. Create a separate referrals section – as against general feedback – in your business so that you can build on these important customers

- Comment positively about complaints and be supportive. Make sure of course about openness and be clear about the action you have taken to resolve the complaint issue.

9   Success breeds success

- Customers like the positive news of success. The validation that someone has been happy with your product is a great encouragement to prospective customers. If you are selling a service you need to be a bit careful here. You should not mention your customer by name unless you have their permission to do so. Also it is better to wait until the service has been delivered before anything is mentioned!
- You can of course mention that you are currently working with a client in a specific sector without mentioning the client's name or location.
- Broadcast success to the world. Create a platform of social media and website updates to let your market place know that you are succeeding
- Involve staff/colleagues who have contributed. Your success may not just be down to you. Help in creating a customer focused journey by involving everybody who has been part of that success. Mention them in social media update – let them have some of the glory from a successful customer journey.

10   Reviewing and modifying approach

- Constantly review that what you are doing is right with existing customers. Everybody knows that we are working in a changing world.
- Are you and your product/service still up to date? Are you continuing to win customers?
- Avoid change for changes sake. If there is no evidence of change in the short term and everything is working well, try to avoid change for changes sake.

- Somebody recently said to me that they were changing the supermarket where they shopped because "they continually change their layout and I can't find anything".
- If it is necessary change and tell the world why. If you are keeping up to date make sure people know not only that you are doing this but it is to improve your customer journey. This will help you as part of the process of "winning customers".

YOUR NOTES FROM CHAPTER 6

Chapter 7

Top 10 Tips for optimising the marketing mix

By Jacqueline Griffith

This chapter outlines how to utilise marketing tools to achieve your business goals in your chosen target market. How to combine product, price, channel of distribution and promotion to create a winning combination. It also considers the opportunities and threats from external factors that can influence the business.

1   The Marketing Mix is a combination of:
- Product (or service)
- Pricing
- Place (channel of distribution)
- Promotion

2   What are your key products or services?

- Your product or service will fit one of the product classifications including consumer or industrial, goods or services.

- **Consumer goods**
- Consumer goods include a variety of goods purchased routinely by the public including:
- Convenience goods that form part of our weekly shop.
- Consumer durables include home appliances.
- Speciality goods can be higher value designer goods.
- Unsought goods for example product extended warranties.

- **Industrial goods**

Goods required for industrial companies to run their business and manufacture their goods, including materials and machinery.

- **Consumer services**

Services sold to consumers often include the services of trades' people offering their services to private households including plumbers, electricians and gardeners.

- **Industrial services**

Services provided to industry include cleaning and maintenance services. There are many freelance consultants offering their industry consulting expertise to businesses and anyone offering Personal Administrator services would be included in this category.

New product development
- You may be developing new products or services to bring you into new markets, replace existing products or simply copy other products or services available in the market.
- If you fail to develop new offerings for your customers you might find your current offerings become less desirable over time and you suffer the fate of reduced future revenue. Research the market and do your market testing of any new product or service to ensure market desirability.

Product Lifecycle
- The stages of a product lifecycle are: Introduction, growth, Maturity and Decline hence the need for new product development to replace declining products and services with fresh offerings.
- Beware of **imitation products** that may rival your product. If you have designed a unique product can it be patented to prevent cheap copies? Companies of similar standing in the market arena introduce similar products as they realise there is a ready-made market for these products with relatively low risk.

Product Strategy
- Assuming that you are offering more than one product or service it is worth monitoring the performance of each. For example, if you are providing IT support to legacy systems that are being phased out you may decide to switch your focus to newer systems that will provide you with a more reliable future revenue stream.

3   How will you price your products or services?

Strategic pricing.
- Pricing should be a strategic decision based on all elements of the marketing mix. Consider the following:
- Does your pricing support your marketing objectives?
- Is your pricing consistent with the rest of your marketing mix including your product, channel of distribution and promotion?
- Try to avoid relying on price as the main competitive factor.
- Don't rely on making pricing decisions based on accounting aspects alone.

Economic pricing.
- The four basic laws of supply and demand are:
- If demand increases and supply is unchanged, a shortage will lead to a higher price.
- If demand decreases and supply is unchanged, a surplus will lead to a lower price.
- If demand remains unchanged and supply increases, a surplus will lead to a lower price.
- If demand remains unchanged and supply decreases, a shortage will lead to a higher price.

The game plan is to maximise profit by setting prices that cover costs and deliver good margins but remember this can be affected by changes in demand and supply. Remain vigilant on how demand and supply are affecting your market.

Accounting pricing
- Accountants tend to base their pricing decisions on costs often using a cost plus theory using the variable costs of producing one additional unit plus a proportion of fixed costs (overheads) to reach the break-even point plus a percentage margin to ensure the price set is profitable.

Market pricing

- Given that the upper limit for a price is often dictated by demand and the lower limit by the production costs, you need to decide where to set prices somewhere between these barriers. You can move these barriers by lowering costs or raising the perceived value of the product.
- Market pricing takes into consideration costs, demand, supply, marketing objectives, competition, distributors (agents) and trends.
- You may be new to the market but that does not mean you have to be cheap! New consultants often under value themselves and this is reflected in low fees. As a rough rule of thumb take your corporate salary and benefits package and divide it by 120 for an indication of day rate on the basis that the average number of billable days for a freelance consultant will be around 120 per year but those days have to provide a living for 365 days a year. Do take into consideration other market forces.
- It is unlikely that your business will be a monopoly and will almost certainly have to compete with competitors offering similar products and services in your chosen market. Know your enemy. Research and check what your **competitors** are offering, at what price and on which terms. This is easier to do before you launch your business and they realise you are a competitor! You can always ask some of your contacts to obtain quotes from competitors for you.
- You can find yourself in the middle of a **price war** when companies continuously lower prices to undercut the competition. It is a quick way to increase revenue in the short term or as a longer term strategy to gain market share but at the risk of erosion of margins. We have seen this in the supermarket chains.

Policies & Procedures for Discounts

- While setting pricing levels remember to set your credit policies and procedures for offering discounts for quantity or early payment.

4   Which channels of distribution do you intend to use to distribute your products or services to reach your target market?

- **Sell directly** to your customers with no middle man involved.
- Use an intermediary, for example find your customers through an **agent**. Contractors often use agents that introduce them to companies requiring their skills for a fixed term.
- Using **multiple channels** of distribution for example via producer, wholesaler and retailer to consumer.
- **Reverse channels** rely on goods moving from consumers to users, for example the resale of second hand goods or recycling.
- The level of **market exposure** you require will influence your choice of channel of distribution. For intense exposure use as many outlets as possible, for exclusivity you may decide to appoint specialist dealers.
- In an ideal world you should be aiming for customer centric service that meets customer requirements at minimum distribution cost.

5   How will you promote your products or services?

- Decide on your **communications strategy** based on accessing your target market, information required by customers, communications objectives, costs and available budget.
- Set out your **communications objectives**. Are you informing the market about a new product, introducing offers or building company image.

- Think practically about your **communications practice**. If customers are making decisions in store then your point-of-sale material is important, however, if you are selling a technical product this lends itself to direct sales, particularly for tailored products and services.
- **Non media promotion** is conducted by your company including: direct mail, door to door selling and location marketing (sandwich boards work well for small local businesses).
- Your public reputation is important to any business so consider how you are going to use **public relations** to maintain the right image. Does your company support a local charity? Do your customers know that?
- Media **advertising** can be costly so if you decide to use it make sure the media you are using will reach your chosen target market or it is a waste of money.
- Modern marketing methods utilise **digital marketing** using the internet on personal computers and smart phones to promote products and services using websites, social media sites, email and apps; in addition to the non-internet options of TV, radio and SMS. This can be a very cost effective way to promote your business.

Note: To learn more about digital marketing please refer to our sister book "100+ Top Tips for Effectively Using Social Media" available in this series.

- **Personal selling** can be a very effective method of promotion, particularly for technical products or services but it comes at a price so make sure your sales people generate revenue in excess of their costs. The typical selling process includes: opening contact, customer needs analysis, constructing and presenting a solution, dealing with objections, negotiating and closing the deal.

- Selling is very straight forward, the key is understanding what the customer wants and then translating that into a product or service solution to meet the customer's operational, technical and budget requirements, then asking for the order!
- In small businesses often sales and **sales management** fall on the owner. Whether you are employing sales people or doing it yourself then you will need to manage the process: setting sales targets and strategy, recruiting people with the right knowledge, skills and experience, then motivating, training and controlling performance (or developing your own sales skills).

6   Have you completed your SWOT Analysis?

- In corporate life you would expect a business to conduct an assessment of the company's Strengths, Weaknesses, Opportunities and Threats. You may take the view that this is not necessary for a small business but remember your business is an investment of your time, effort and money so the SWOT analysis is worth a little consideration.

- **Strengths** – what will make your business offering a compelling proposition in your market?
- **Weaknesses** – what puts your business offering at a disadvantage in your chosen market?
- **Opportunities** – Where will future sales opportunities come from? What market changes could play to your advantage?
- **Threats** – Be market savvy to be aware of changes that could impact negatively on your business.

- Changes that can impact your business either positively or negatively are: Political, Economic, Social and Technical. A flavour of some of these issues is detailed below:

7 What potential political or economic changes could impact your business?

- Political change particularly through the introduction of new legislation, can impact on your business both positively and negatively. If you work in a highly regulated industry new regulations or compliance may introduce the need for greater training, administration and investment.
- Deregulation can open up a previously unattainable market; however, it could introduce competitors to what was previously a very lucrative market.
- You may remember the introduction of the Home Information Pack (HIP) in 2007 as a requirement for anyone selling their home. This legislation was abolished in 2010 as the government was concerned that the increased cost and hassle was stifling a fragile housing market. A supplier of HIP elements to HIP Inspectors stated that he would have to completely change the company's business model overnight.
- Consumer law and protection is constantly being improved by the UK government affecting products and services provided to consumers. If your target market is consumers stay up to date with these changes.

Credit
- Pre the global credit crash of 2008 there was almost unlimited credit available. Economic forces certainly did affect businesses as a result of the tightening of credit; many small businesses complained that their banks withdrew their bank overdrafts devastating their cash flow position.

Unemployment level
- Rising unemployment levels can lower consumer spending, increase the demand for lower priced goods, lower wages, create work insecurity, recruitment becomes easier, lower staff turnover and the reverse is true of falling unemployment.

Inflation rate

- Inflation is a rise in prices and a fall in the value of money measured by the government as the Retail Price Index (RPI) against a representative basket of goods.
- Rising inflation can cause rising interest rates, rising materials and labour costs and affect price competitiveness for overseas trade.

Fiscal policies

- Fiscal policy is the government's spending and taxation practices. Lower taxes and higher government spending can generate greater disposable income and consumer spending.

8 Are there social trends that could tip the balance in your favour?

Fashions

- Seasonal fashions can help to predict consumer buying habits.

Tastes

- Changes in consumer tastes can affect the demand for products for example a leaning towards food safety, healthier eating and more active lifestyle.

Demographic factors.

- Changes in the demographic mix can affect demand; take for example an aging population in the UK and the increased value of the "grey pound" through the spending power of wealthier older people.

Trends

- Factors we have already discussed can become trends keep an eye on the trends that are likely to affect your business.
- Changing customer needs will affect product or service usage.

- Pricing changes with a trend to discounting.

- Technology with the increasing use of online purchasing.
- Social factors for example a rise in networking.
- Communications/media such as increased use of social media.
- Global factors can affect changes in the world economy.

9   Can you embrace technical innovation and environmental issues to your advantage?

- **Online retailing** – Enabling customers to order and pay for goods on your website.
- **Digital marketing** using social media please refer to our sister book "100+ Top Tips for Effectively Using Social Media" in this series.
- **Mobile applications** – There is a surge in companies offering mobile applications that simplify the way customers interact with that supplier.
- **Text reminder messages** – To avoid customers forgetting their appointment with you; send them a text reminding them. My hairdresser calls me by telephone the day before my appointment to remind me of the time of my appointment.
- **Automation** of production processes – Can you embrace the introduction of robotics within your production processes to reduce the production cost per unit?
- Apart from meeting legislation there can be opportunities to boost your market share from embracing green sustainable business practices and a willingness to promote these practices.
- **Recycling** – Is your product / packaging suitable for recycling? Do you recycle your waste paper?
- **Biodegradable** – Is your product / packaging biodegradable?
- **Disposal** of industrial waste - Do your practices meet regulations and the ethics of your business? Contamination can have a damaging effect on your reputation.

10   Managing the Marketing Mix

- **Setting marketing objectives**.
  This is easier when you have a year of trading behind you with some historical data to analyse, however, at the set-up of your business you will need to rely on whole market figures and an estimate of what proportion of that market you may secure, giving consideration to opportunities and threats from trends and changes mentioned in points 7-12 in this chapter. Make sure your objectives are quantified or you will be unable to measure success at the end of the year.
- **Choosing marketing strategies**.
  Strategy is a medium to long term overview including: deciding on a target market, market positioning and the marketing mix. By comparison marketing tactics are more detailed, shorter term and flexible for example a price promotion to move some stock.
- **Preparing the annual marketing plan**.
  Create a marketing plan of what the business will sell, to whom, when and how. Start with a situation analysis of current sales and profit trends (if you have any recent trading figures), total market size, competitor and market share analysis, not forgetting external factors and how they may impact on the business in the coming year. Financials will include your sales projections and budgeted costs. State the marketing strategy and marketing mix that will be adopted.

YOUR NOTES FROM CHAPTER 7

Chapter 8

Top 10 Tips for product or service operations delivery

By Ian Munro

The impact of this not working affects the Customer Journey mentioned earlier. Getting this piece wrong will impact on their journey, getting it right will save you costs that otherwise will incur. To some readers this may seem complicated. From our experience at the pace business moves today you need to be ready to handle the unexpected.

1   **What are the expected/accepted standard service levels?**

- How do your suppliers operate? It's no good you having an expectation of their timescales, services and prices if you have not checked out what are the general standards about how these suppliers operate. Your misinterpretation could have a significant impact on your subsequent supply of goods or services to your customers.
- How do your competitors operate? If competitor products are normally delivered within 36 hours, why should your customers be expected to wait longer than this time?
- What are customer expectations? Managing customer expectations are key. Have you clear statements about delivery?

2   **Creating the delivery process/journey**
- Model the journey for a product and/or services delivery accepting that we are at the fulfilment stage. We have previously discussed the complete customer journey from enquiry stage. Now we are looking at what can be called the "fulfilment" stage. This is where something actually happens. Either a products gets delivered – this includes the download of an app or other software – as well as you being a subject specialist delivering consultancy advice or say a training programme.
- If you are delivering a product consider storage, handling and distribution.

- You will already have decided whether you are doing all the physical handling or are you subcontracting that part of your business to a sub contracted third party. Have you agreed with the supplier your customer delivery/process journey?
- If delivering a service what are the timelines and are associates involved. If you are working with associates it is equally key at the delivery stage that they know of the expectations of your customer at this point of the process.

3   How will you meet the expected service levels

- Test the process with dummy orders. Have several trials with dummy orders to validate the delivery stage works. Do this a few times a month to make sure the model continues to work.
- Look closely for logjams. The easiest way to do this is to check on any pattern changes to goods received dates against projected delivery dates.
- Create fall back solutions. Set up contingency plans for alternatives in the event of a large number of delivery failures. From a goods perspective, by having two regular delivery companies, if one fails you have another. Likewise if you are say running a training programme, share it between two or three of you so that if someone is ill the programme does not need to be cancelled.

4   Creating supplier terms and conditions

- Create your procurement T & Cs. You should set up your terms and condition for procurement (buying) goods and services. These can be downloaded from the internet. If working with associates make sure you have an associate's agreement and that they countersign any contact letter with your client where they agree to be bound by the same terms and conditions.

- Negotiate payment terms. In the early days your good may have to be paid for in advance. Sometimes a supplier will allow you to open an account but with strict monthly payment terms
- Identify preferred suppliers. Agree where you can that two or three suppliers will be your preferred supplier and in exchange for this you want preferential payment terms.
- If stock is involved look at Just In Time. Stock holding nowadays is greatly reduced as stock ties up cash that is needed elsewhere in your business. The first step mentioned above is preferred suppliers and with them you should be negotiating a fast turn round or orders. A good example is where you order by 14.00 one working day the order will be delivered before 12.00 the next working day.

5   Building checks and controls

- Check quality of goods and services meet the customer expectation. If receiving goods for immediate despatch to customers, make spot checks on all received goods to check you are receiving exactly what you ordered. If delivering a service, get confirmation from the customer that they are getting what they expected.
- Delivery schedules should show expected and actual delivery dates. Keep a record of these so that you can have early notification if something is slipping.
- Pricing changes need to be considered. If supplier prices change or shipping costs are increased, these will eat straight into your profit margins. Make sure you are ready to respond where this occurs.

6   Building supplier relationships

- Treat them like customers. Without your suppliers you will have no customers, so establishing good levels of dialogue with your suppliers is key.

- Aim to motivate them just as you would your staff. Make sure they are praised when they give you a high level of response or service. If providing a service your associates are representing you. Keep them involved and updated on developments. If you are able to give them an income stream, they will want to work with you.
- Open up clear communication channels. Agree Service Level Agreements (SLAs) with your suppliers. This is the only fair way to measure expectations and performance. Create a two way "hotline" for fast response with issues and challenges. With associates have an associates' agreement which spells out how you will operate.
- Have fortnightly/monthly review meetings. The timing will depend on the frequency and volume of your business. It is good practice to review a service with suppliers whatever your business. This needn't be face to face you can always use Skype or a similar service to have a webcam call.

7   Building customer relationships

- Open up clear communication channels. Just like with suppliers we are saying exactly the same here. Agree Service Level Agreements (SLAs) with your customers. This is the only fair way to measure their expectations and your performance. Create a two way "hotline" for fast response with issues and challenges. With associates have an associates' agreement which spells out how you will operate.
- Constantly ask for satisfaction feedback. In product based businesses as well as services it is good practice to ask for a satisfaction update on a regular basis. This reaffirms that the customer is satisfied with progress.
- Set up fortnightly/monthly review meetings. Again we are copying the same message from above. The timing will depend on the frequency and volume of your business. It is good practice to review a service with customers whatever your business.

- This needn't be face to face you can always use Skype or a similar service to have a webcam call.

8   Consider the financial implications

- Cash is king! A well-known statement but cash really is the lifeblood that runs through your venture. Product sales may be made via credit cards if the customer is a consumer but businesses will expect to open an account. Until a credit check – via your bank or related source – can be made on your customer even trade customers may have to buy via credit card. Selling services to businesses rarely involves credit card and customers may want to see delivery of the service before handing over money. You can still request payment in 14 days from date of delivery.
- Are you at risk from margin erosion? Unless you have trade discounts or volume discounts built into your pricing plan, do not give away sales margin. Sales margin is what pays the business overheads and eventually a profit for the business. All businesses need to make profit some of which will be reinvested. Margin erosion means you cannot afford to do this.
- Stock ties up cash. We have mentioned Just in Time arrangements with suppliers to reduce your stock holding. Some organisations end up with unused stock at the end of a project. Make sure that all the materials you ordered were a component part of your costing for the project and costed into the project. Sometimes you can sell back unused components to suppliers releasing more cash into the business.

9   Keeping abreast of market changes

- Identify trends of changes in product or service delivery. We are not just looking at warehousing and delivery here.

- Are there different ways that those in your sector are delivering services? Are products being made with new components? Will either of these impact on your overall delivery of a product or service?
- Keep involved in sector events. Either through local trade bodies or regional branches of a professional body you can be kept updated on forthcoming legislation changes, or new product and services developments. All of this can be a blend of being there or updating yourself by journals or the web.
- Get customer views. Customers are keen to be using the latest equipment or technology. However, they will not always be prepared to pay an increase in price. However, they too want to keep abreast of changes so encourage them to have an information exchange with you.

10   Investing in equipment and technology

- From materials handling to software. Your product/service delivery is likely to involve you in technology updates. This can be as simple as having to pay more for components which embody the latest technology. You may have packing or manufacturing equipment where an investment will bring an almost immediate improvement in margin.
- When to make the change will depend on a number of factors. Sometimes the suppliers' changes have teething and general bedding in issues. This could impact further down line on your customers who will blame you. We recommend that you only get involved in new technology and processes when you are satisfied that the trial phase has been completed.
- Where there is clear evidence that changes will improve service/product profit and will have an immediate impact then clearly this becomes a decision issue.

- Your prime responsibility is to deliver an exceptional level of service to customers whilst enhancing the profitability of your business. You are not there to be a beacon and trendsetter for your sector at large.

YOUR NOTES FROM CHAPTER 8

Chapter 9

Top 10 Tips for employing staff or working with Associates

By Jacqueline Griffith

This section covers the detail of recruiting staff and engaging Associates. It is intended to give the reader some pointers and areas to be considered. Regulations in this area are constantly changing so you need to keep abreast of planned and actual changes to employment legislation

1   Recruiting staff

- Before recruiting a member of staff it is worth writing a job description including the responsibilities and duties of the role together with the essential and desirable, knowledge, skills and experience required for someone to be a good fit for the job.
- Decide how much you are going to pay. This needs to be at least the national minimum rate and ideally in line with market rates for the job so do your research on pay rates for similar jobs.
- Many jobs are filled through personal contacts, a great way to find good people with a known track record without paying agents or advertising fees so network with your contacts.
- It is worth advertising any jobs you wish to fill on your own company website so when you build the website remember to include a section for careers.
- Recruitment agents are fee income generating so do be mindful of this when appointing an agent. Brief the agent with a job description, set a response time for CVs, ask for 5-8 screened good quality CVs, explain the number of interviews candidates will need to attend as part of your recruitment process and state if there will be any assessment tests. Make a verbal offer via the agent, once accepted confirm salary and benefits in writing.
- Advertising is often expensive and if not targeted can bring a deluge of inappropriate applicants.

- If you do advertise to recruit ensure you include the main responsibilities of the role, plus the essential and desirable knowledge, skills and experience required of successful candidates to narrow the response.
- As an employer it is your legal obligation to avoid discrimination when you recruit. Adverts should avoid any reference to age, sex, race, religion, parental status, or other characteristics protected by law unless by specific exception e.g. over 18 to serve alcohol.

2   Contract of Employment

- You can employ people on very different contractual arrangements not necessarily on a permanent contract basis. You should provide employees with a contract of employment stating their terms of employment, which you both abide by until the contract ends usually by one party serving notice.
- Full time and part time contracts – these contracts provide security of employment for a pre-determined number of hours on an ongoing basis and usually include a notice period.
- Fixed term contracts are useful if you need to employ someone for a set number of months, usually 3-12 months with no ongoing commitment beyond the contracted period.
- Agency staff tend to be supplied on an agency PAYE basis where the agent recruits and employs staff on a temporary basis and invoices you monthly based on the hours worked.
- Freelancers, Consultants and Contractors supplying their expertise to your business on an ad hoc basis usually do so invoicing you for their services through their own business.
- Zero hours contracts offer employers the flexibility of employing people with no minimum working hours but neither is there any obligation on the employee to accept any hours offered.

3   Statutory entitlement – subject to change

- Holiday pay – Full time employees are nominally entitled to 5.6 weeks paid leave per year including bank holidays so remember to consider if you need staff to work on the bank holidays.
- Sick pay - If your staff are sick you will need to pay them Statutory Sick Pay for up to 28 weeks, however, many companies offer enhanced sick pay arrangements as part of their benefits package.
- Maternity and paternity pay – employees can take up to 52 weeks maternity leave. Statutory Maternity is paid for up to 39 weeks. Check the Government website for guidelines on benefits.
- Jury service – Your employees have a right to time off for Jury Service but you can delay it once in 12 months, for example if it is your peak season and you cannot manage without that employee's expertise during that period.

4   Health and Safety

- Taking simple precautions on health and safety can save you a great deal of unnecessary grief so write a Health and Safety policy for your business.
- The Health and Safety Executive (HSE) provide a great deal of guidance for businesses on their website www.hse.gov.uk
- Conduct a risk assessment and consider if staff need training or protective clothing if they are using machinery.
- Identify fire risk areas including: storage of flammable liquids, hazardous operation, type of fire extinguisher required, site accessibility for fire response teams and nearest fire hydrant.
- Smoke-free legislation has been introduced in England, Scotland Wales and Northern Ireland banning smoking in nearly all enclosed workplaces.

- As an employer you need to display 'no smoking' signs in all workplaces and vehicles and make sure people don't smoke in enclosed work premises or shared vehicles or face hefty fines.
- As a business owner you have a duty of care to ensure your business minimises waste, optimises recycling and avoids polluting the environment. You could promote this Eco virtue as part of your business social responsibility policy.

5   Training

- Create an Induction Training plan for new employees.
- Job related training is a tax deductible business expense.
- Training does not have to be in a classroom it can be supervised on the job training or by observation of experienced employees.
- Train an experienced member of staff as a trained trainer and they can deliver internal training for a fraction of the cost of paying external trainers.

6   Payroll

- New employers should register online with HM Revenue and Customs (HMRC) for PAYE company registration when you start employing staff.
- If you are going to do the PAYE tax and National Insurance Contributions calculations yourself you may wish to buy some PAYE software. It is worth checking that the software you use is compatible with the HMRC website software and if you only employ 9 or less employees you can download some free PAYE software form the HMRC website.
- Employers are required to deduct Income Tax from your employees' salary and pay this over to HMRC via your internal or outsourced payroll function.

- The NIC deductions for staff include class 1 NIC paid by employees and Employers' NIC paid by your business.
- NIC for directors are worked out from their annual earnings rather than from what they earn in each pay period. There are two methods for this depending on whether regular or irregular salary payments are made to the Director. Employers' NIC contributions are also deductible on director's salaries.
- Benefits in kind that you provide your employees with are also taxable for example private medical health insurance.
- If you provide company cars or fuel for your employees' private use, you need to calculate the taxable value based on the fuel type and CO_2 emissions and report this to HMRC.

7   Pensions

- The government are phasing in the requirement for all businesses to provide an auto enrolment pension scheme for qualifying staff with specified minimum employer contributions.
- Employees will have the option to opt out but you should budget for all staff to remain in the scheme.
- Employees can agree to salary sacrifice in exchange for putting a contribution into their company pension, this should reduce the NIC payments for both the employer and employee.
- Small businesses that do not meet their auto-enrolment obligations can be hit with punitive fines.

8   Disciplinary and Grievance procedures

- There is value in writing a disciplinary and Grievance procedure including a right of appeal.
- When issues arise either from the employee's or employer's aspect there is a clear code of practice in place.

- The rules should follow the ACAS (Advisory, Conciliation and Arbitration Service) code of practice on disciplinary and grievance procedures.
- Set standards of performance for staff so they are aware of what is expected of them.
- Deal with disciplinary and grievance issues early, interview employees to gain their view and what support they feel they need to get them back on track, offer employees the opportunity to be accompanied in the meeting.
- Keep records of all meetings and written notifications.

9   Redundancy

- The single biggest complaint I hear from people when their jobs are at risk of redundancy is the lack of communication from their employer. If a whole department is affected then make an announcement to all staff in that department with an indication of timescales. Interview each individual affected by the change to discuss their options and the financial implications for them.
- Support your staff with an outplacement service, there are so many benefits to this: a committed workforce during a period of change, positive view of your business when they leave and evangelise what a great company they were a part of and positivity from unaffected staff who otherwise may suffer survivor syndrome.
- Can you redeploy staff in new roles with some retraining? Potentially saving money on recruitment and redundancy costs.
- Non-Compulsory redundancy. Often staff can present you with solutions that you had not considered for example voluntary severance or early retirement which may reduce the number of compulsory redundancies.

- Consultation. There are guidelines for the consultation process given the number of jobs that are affected. Ensure you work within the appropriate collective consultation period.
- Following consultation, when you serve notice, ensure you provide a letter stating the termination date, financial settlement and any additional support available.
- Redundancy payments. Make sure these are timely and correct it is the final insult to anyone leaving to find their final pay settlement is inaccurate.

10   Working with Associates

- Working with freelance consultants on an associate basis is a common business model. Giving you access to expertise that would be high cost to carry on your permanent head count with the luxury of only using and paying for that resource for specific deliveries. Typically Associates will invoice their delivery time on a monthly basis on pre- agreed terms.
- This model is an effective method of coping with volatility in business demand whilst minimising fixed costs.
- Associates can provide specialist expertise at softer rates as a result of the regularity of work provided.
- The upside for Associates is the attraction of improved "work / life balance" and the opportunity to have a "portfolio career".
- As an individual, you can operate as an Associate with one or more organisations but beware of associate agreements that include an exclusivity clause; this can restrict you from working for competing businesses in your chosen sector.

YOUR NOTES FROM CHAPTER 9

Chapter 10

Top 10 Tips for keeping records, paying taxes and dealing with advisers

By Ian Munro

Keeping records are not just an obvious part of running a business. There are many regulations that require up to date records to be maintained. If you fail to meet the required standards you will be at risk of substantial fines. Keep updated about changes that may affect your business.

For instance GDPR. The General Data Protection Regulation came into effect on 25th May 2018. It is in fact a straightforward process provided that you understand how to make your website GDPR compliant. You can find some basic information in the Learning Zone.

Note: Some of this chapter's content can be read in greater detail in our sister book 100 + Top Tips for understanding Business Finance

1   Cash, Sales invoices and Supplier invoices

Cash

- This is the third time we have said that "Cash is King" and this applies to large international organisations as well as small one to five people ventures. Cash is the life blood of a business. If heaven forbid you suffered a serious blood loss your life would be in real danger, so you would need to take immediate urgent action to resolve this problem. If your business is losing cash it will be in exactly the same position as you so what can you do?
- Firstly, you can do nothing unless you have current bang up to date projections on your current cash position. This includes looking at who owes you money and when are you likely to get paid. Also what suppliers are you due to pay and when are they expecting to get paid?
- We recommend that you look at your actual and projected cash position daily.

- Do not give this task to someone else – this is one of your prime tasks. So how do you administrate this, what records do you keep?
- Some people I know simply work off a number of spreadsheets and very effectively manage their cash this way.
- A practical option for those new to running their own venture is to run a small PC based bookkeeping software package which integrates with your bank account.
- Most of these systems will work in real time so you will know very quickly if you have a problem looming. If you do not have the two linked then at least weekly do a reconciliation between what the systems says is in your bank account with your actual bank account. If variances start to appear, find out immediately why this is the case.

Sales Invoices

- I met a business owner recently and when I asked about what his biggest challenge was they said "finding the time to raise invoices. Sometimes I am up to two weeks late" All this tells me is that the time between delivering a product or service to getting ultimately paid will eventually impact on his cash position. People who buy goods or services do expect to pay so why make life easy for them.
- We recommend that you invoice at least twice per week and enter that activity in your calendar so that you do not forget.
- However, depending on the complexities of your business you may not need an accounting package for your invoicing. One of our fellow writers in this book series raises 1000 invoices a week – he needs a heavily automated process.

- Some of our colleagues who are supplying a professional service may only have about six invoices a month, so they need a simple process.
- An example of an invoicing log can be seen in the Learning Zone and this will certainly meet your basic "early days" needs.

Supplier invoices

- As has been said elsewhere your suppliers - be they associate colleagues or suppliers of goods are essential to the running of your business. As with the Sales Invoicing log you will find one for suppliers. In an ideal world you will want to delay payments until you at least have been paid for by your customer for the goods or services provided. This means you need to carefully read their Terms and Conditions before placing an order or contract with them. It is quite normal to negotiate not just on price but payment terms too.
- We have worked with a wholesaler who generally managed their cash by expecting maximum customer payment in 35 days and they paid suppliers in 45 days
- All these three areas are closely entwined – your cash position, sales invoicing and supplier invoicing, so keeping at least some of the basic records we suggest will help you to stay on top of things. Just note that every business needs to grow to survive, so your managing of these areas needs to be able to keep pace with business growth.

2   Contact Plan

- In the early days you will be doing a balancing act with your time.

- This will be between the three main functional drivers; marketing and sales, operations and fulfilment, finance and legal. You will be meeting people in all three areas and need an overall system for not just short term contact but over the middle to longer term too.
- We have found with others who have asked us for advice that if you are not careful you will find your activities being driven by others and not you.
- Whilst making sure that your customers are getting the service they thought they were buying you are running a business which has other needs too. So you need to have a sense of balance in what you do to make sure across the board objectives are met.
- This is why we have created a Contact Plan which has an example in the Learning Zone. This tool allows you to plan activities and to keep contact with people in the main three functional areas.

Paying Taxes

3   VAT

- When you register for VAT what you are effectively becoming is a government unpaid tax collector. However one of the upsides of being VAT registered is that under certain schemes you can reclaim the VAT you have paid to suppliers for goods and services.
- The Learning Zone provides a link to where you can find information about registering for VAT, so it is not the intention to go into that detail here. Also there are sometimes minor changes to VAT so it is a good habit to see updates on the HMRC website.
- Just a quick note here. There is a threshold – currently £85,000 annual turnover - when you are legally required to register for VAT. Many of my colleagues have a "voluntary" registration which you will get if you are trading as this allows you to reclaim the VAT on purchases.

- Finally do not let anyone tell you that producing a VAT return is a complex issue. I do two returns once a quarter myself which together take me about 1.5 hours – provided your ongoing information is up to date it is not difficult. An example of the form I created is in the Learning Zone.

4   Corporation Tax

- All business in the UK must pay Corporation Tax on the profits made by the business. By profits we mean sales less cost of sales less the overhead costs of running the business.
- Here we are exploring the basics and again in the Learning Zone you will find the links to a number of questions you may have on the HMRC web site.
- Generally speaking I recommend that 20% of your projected profit be put on one side as the time will come after the end of an accounting period when this money will be due to HMRC.

5   Personal Tax

- It is probably seeming now that you are becoming a collector of taxes for the government! Funnily enough this has not changed – as an employee you were paying regular taxes for different issues but these were not so visible to you as the collection was done through your employer's payroll system. Two different taxes come into play here as shown below.
- Income Tax and National Insurance. At his stage the water gets a bit muddy because everyone has their own situation in terms of their personal funding needs and sources of income that can come from different areas – investments and savings as well as employment. All of these will have a different impact on the reader's tax liability.

- Personally, I have always retained a small business accountant to look after my tax affairs and related issues. Not because I am wealthy – which I am not – but because these can be complex areas and the worst thing you can do is end up not taking advantage of grants and allowances ending up paying more tax than you need to.
- As a general statement, every year my accountant has worked with me he has saved me more than what he charges. However please do not tell him this or he might just increase his fees!

Dealing with Advisors

6   Accountants

- You will generally find a number of possible accountants via referrals from others who have previously taken this same step.
- Do not be tempted into a snap decision, a phone call with a prospective accountant is not good. Go and meet at least three and then you will have a choice to decide on which one you can work with.
- Keep your costs down by doing basic tasks yourself: invoicing, VAT returns.
- If you are a director in your own company you do not need to have PAYE. You can have your accountant produce a P60 at the year-end as he prepares your accounts
- Some accountants like to charge on a monthly basis. For example for a simple small transactions company it could cost £750 p.a. with a further £200 to do your personal tax. Some accountants like to charge you say £80 per month to cover this. When my accountant does some work for me I pay him rather than paying him in advance of any work done.

7   Legal

- There are times when you may need some legal advice and therefore it could be good practice to listen out for who others consider to be a good commercial lawyer when you do general networking.
- The good law practices I work with will take a brief from me and then give an accurate projection about costs for that brief.
- The legal scene has changed quite dramatically in the last few years and gone are the days when many got caught out with ever increasing and unexpected legal bills. However please take note that the initial clearly focused briefing session – which should be free to you - is where is all begins.

8   Subject Matter Experts

- You may well be a Subject Matter Expert yourself? Certainly in whatever you plan to do in your business I sincerely hope that you are an expert in your chosen area or are taking steps to become one.
- On that basis you would probably object if people constantly contacted you for advice and expect you to give this for nothing?
- On this basis therefore if you agree with what I have said above there will be people/contacts in your network who could be helpful to you. You should offer to pay for this advice, just as you would expect to be paid for yours.
- As a sort of half-way house, you could offer people some help on the "old pals" basis provided they were prepared to give you some contacts and information that would be helpful to you.

9 Mentors

- There is a growing trend for people to use Coaches and Mentors in their workplace.
- It can be a lonely old place sitting at the top of your venture so to have others with whom you can either seek advice or general guidance has many benefits from sound boarding on your options to specific help in resolving a key issue.
- Generally, mentors are established experts in a field of expertise. This could be general or function specific.
- Often in an organisation they will be a senior executive working in a related part of the business. Most mentors based on their experience will offer solutions to the mentee.
- There are also independent Mentors who are not employed in an organisation – they effectively run their own mentoring business.

10 Coaches

- A coach will preferably be independent to the organisation. Some organisations have a team of internal coaches.
- However in our experience with the best possible intent senior executives are reluctant to share some of the issues they wish to discuss with an internal coach.
- The key difference between the mentor and the coach is that a coach will not come up with solutions and options.
- The coach will lead the discussions in such a way that the coachee will identify the solution and in this way will have full ownership of their options.

- A collectively good point about Mentors and Coaches is that their service can be obtained on a session by session basis that would normally be 1.5 or 2 hour sessions over a four to six month period.
- A list of coach and mentor organisations can be found in the Learning Zone.

YOUR NOTES FROM CHAPTER 10

Summary

We hope that you will have found this book of real benefit.

As stated in the Introduction this is one of the first clear guides about how to set up and run a new business in plain English with pragmatic tips.

I mentioned before that feedback from clients and readers helps me to further fine tune our material, so please keep the emails coming

Our best wishes to you all.

Ian Munro   **Jacqueline Griffith**

feedback.ownbusiness@100toptips.com

About the Authors

Ian Munro has been helping people set up businesses and working with businesses going through periods of sustained growth for over 20 years. He works as an operating and main board director, as a non-executive director and as a consultant, coach and mentor. His clients are in the private and public sectors. An ongoing feature of his work is improving leadership performance across all levels in organisations. Today he continues to hold several directorships.

Jacqueline Griffith has been coaching new entrepreneurs from business set up to developing successful businesses for over 15 years. Her corporate background is in Director level and General Manager roles encompassing sales, operations and logistics. Her experience includes the merger of five companies and the restructure of two. She adopts a motivational style to encourage people to believe in their ability to start their own business.

Learning Zone

1   Chapter 2 – Tip 10

Decision making process chart

2   Chapter 2 – Tip 5

Customer requirement Analysis

3   Chapter 5 – Tip 1

Profit and Loss template

4   Chapter 5 – Tip 2

Cash flow forecast

5   Chapter 6 – Tip 7

Becoming a great networker

6   Chapter 10 – Heading

General Data Protection Regulation - GDPR

7   Chapter 10 - Tip 1

Invoicing log

8   Chapter 10 – Tip 3

Vat compilation form

1   **Chapter 2 – Tip 10**

Decision making process chart

Seven-step model for strategic decision-making:

1. **Define the problem**

2. **Gather relevant information**

3. **Identify the alternatives**

4. **Weigh the evidence**

5. **Select an alternative**

6. **Implement the alternative**

7. **Evaluate the decision effectiveness**.

2   Chapter 3 – Tip 5

Customer Requirement Analysis

CUSTOMER REQUIREMENT ANALYSIS

Company Name					
Address					
Telephone/Mobile		Email			
Nature of Business					
Products/Services					
Contacts Decisionmaker/ Senior influencers	Name	1	2		3
	Title				
	Email				
Functional Contacts	Operational Users		Technical Specialists		
Technical specification					
Operational Requirements					
Response Times					
Buying Criteria	1				
	2				
	3				
Existing Supplier Satisfaction					
Additional Information Required					
Actions/ Timescales					
Credit approval					
Sales Operations Process	Enquiry	Quote	Negotiation	Order	Invoice	Cust. Service

FILENAME:CUSREQFORM

3 Chapter 5 – Tip 1

Profit and Loss template

PROFIT & LOSS TEMPLATE: TURNOVER BELOW £77,000

Profit and Loss for the YE XX	Month 1	Month 2	Month 3	Month 4	Month 5	Month 6	Month 7	Month 8	Month 9	Month 10	Month 11	Month 12	YTD
Sales	650	6,500	1,000	200	400	800	350	400	780	5,000	600	450	17,130
Other business income	20	20	20	20	20	20	20	20	20	20	20	20	240
Total turnover	670	6,520	1,020	220	420	820	370	420	800	5,020	620	470	17,370
Cost of goods bought for resale or goods used	300	200	400	300	500	600	700	800	900	400	220	200	5,500
Total cost of sales	300	200	400	300	500	600	700	600	900	400	220	200	5,550
Gross Profit	370	6,320	620	−80	−80	220	−330	−380	−100	4,620	420	270	11,870
Car, van and travel expense	400	400	400	400	400	400	400	400	400	400	400	400	4,800
Wages, salaries and other staff costs	120	120	120	120	120	120	120	120	120	120	120	120	1,440
Rent, rates, power and insurance costs	240	240	240	240	240	240	240	240	240	240	240	240	2,880
Repairs and renewals of property and equipment	100	100	100	100	100	100	100	100	100	100	100	100	1,200
Accountancy, legal and other professional fees	100	100	100	100	100	100	100	100	100	100	100	100	1,200
Interest and bank and credit card etc. financial charges	10	10	10	10	10	10	10	10	10	10	10	10	120
Phone, fax, stationery and other office costs	3	3	3	3	3	3	3	3	3	3	3	3	36
Total allowable expenses	973	973	973	973	973	973	973	973	973	973	973	973	11,676
Net profit/(loss)	−603	5,347	−353	−1,053	−1,053	−753	−1,303	−1,353	−1,073	3,647	−553	−703	194

4   Chapter 5 – Tip 2

Cash flow forecast

Monthly Cashflow Forecast
Business Name
Year Ended XX/XX/XX

	Month 1 Forecast	Month 2 Forecast	Month 3 Forecast	Month 4 Forecast	Month 5 Forecast	Month 6 Forecast	Month 7 Forecast	Month 8 Forecast	Month 9 Forecast	Month 10 Forecast	Month 11 Forecast	Month 12 Forecast	Total
Cash receipts													
Cash sales													
Cash collected from debtors													
Other income													
Loan or other cash introduced													
Sales of assets													
Total cash inflow													
Cash cost of sales													
Purchases/Materials													
Total cost of sales													
Cash expenditure													
Salaries/wages													
PAYE/NI													
Lease payments													
Commissions													
Repairs and maintenance													
Office supplies													
Advertising & promotions													
External services													
Vehicle costs													
Travelling													
Accounting													
Legal costs													
Professional services													
Rent													
Council tax													
Water rates													
Telephone													
Utilities													
Insurance													
Interest													
Bank charges													
VAT/(VAT)													
Corporation tax													
Other taxes													
Sundry expenses													
Total expenditure													
Cash capital payments													
Dividends													
Loan repayments													
Assets purchased													
Drawings													
Total capital payments													
Total cash outflow													
Opening balance													
Net cash receipts/(expenditure)													
Closing balance													

5   Chapter 6 – Tip7

Becoming a great networker

We are giving quite a bit of space to this Learning Zone item. This is because almost all the people we know who run their own businesses are successful networkers and networking is something they do all of the time.

1   Remember the four pillars of successful networking

The four pillars of networking are aimed at enhancing your chances of having a successful networking meeting:
1.1 Be non-threatening/ non-selling in your approach
1.2 Ask for more contacts to extend your network
1.3 Take no more than 35/45 minutes for a networking chat
1.4 Offer to help the other party with contacts and/or information

Here's how you do it!

1.1 If someone contacts you and says they would like to have a coffee and a chat, the initial impression is that they want to "sell" you something. So not surprisingly the common reaction is that you can almost hear the shutters coming down. Avoid this by being upfront with a statement like", I am looking for nothing other than your advice. I am at a cross roads in terms of direction and your advice and comments as a sounding board would be invaluable".

1.2 If you don't get more contacts through networking, you are not networking! Try this statement "I am trying to extend my contacts – I am not looking for a "result" from your contacts. The more people who know what I ideally would like to do, the greater the chance of something coming through the grapevine because a networking contact hears about it.

As part of our catch up chat I would welcome some other names of those who you believe can help to widen my network."

1.3 Everyone is time pressurised nowadays. When you ask for a meeting qualify that request with how long you expect to be there. Say for example "If you are able to give me some time, my expectation is that it would be for no more than 35-45 minutes. So I will not be taking up all morning or all afternoon."

1.4 Too many people approach a networking meeting on a me, me, me basis. Networking meetings should be two way. "Getting your comments/advice would be great and in return I would like to be able to help you with contacts and/or information."

2   Always be ready to network

- Even if you are very busy in your job it doesn't mean you cannot network. Too often I hear the plaintive cry "I am too busy to network!"
- If there was some aspect of your job that was essential you would find the time to do it. If networking is essential to your career – as it is – you must find time for it.
- Even if you only have one or two meetings a week – and they could be internal ones – make the space.
- You never know when circumstances may change. In our Career Development work we often meet people who say "I wish I had allocated more time to networking"
- Employment situations change, key people either move out or move away and an opportunity becomes a missed one.
- Change will happen so you need to start networking now!
- You need to keep your network up to date. We have a Contact Plan in the **Learning Zone** which helps you to keep your networking up to date.

- The Contact Plan requires you to plan future networking meetings, which need not be face-to-face - a webcam call is an option.
- Webcam calls are not so good as face-to-face, but are three times better than a phone call and 100 times better than doing nothing.

3   Networking is not selling

- The first bridge you have to cross is realising that networking is not selling.
- If contacts think you are on a sales trip to sell you, they will not be keen to meet.
- Networking is about getting engagement with others who in a non-threatening environment (because you are not selling) are happy to give you their opinions and advice.
- It is a fundamental step in the successful networking process to make it clear when you first phone, in a confirmation email and when you meet to clarify that you are looking for advice and that you value the advice you are likely to get from your contact

4   Be specific about what you would like to achieve

- People like to have bite sized pieces of information to work with.
- When networking, it is good practice to break down the advice you are looking for into no more than three to four bite sized chunks – or headings.
- You can always expand on the headings as you get into the detail.
- The other person may say for example "I understand that you have three main options, let's look at number two. Why did you think your next move should be into the Creative Department?"

- That opens the door for you to go into three to four reasons – maybe less – why the Creative Department is an option.

5   Be welcoming, approachable and easy to talk with

- If you are a dour, unsmiling individual – which I am sure you are not – what impact do you think that will have on people you meet?
- I am not suggesting that you should be an over the top smiley person whose over enthusiasm for everything in life is more likely to put people off than encouraging them to help you.
- Having an open welcoming approach will make you more acceptable to others.
- On the easy to talk with comment, always have an open question ready for people. Open questions require an answer, closed questions get "yes" or "no" answers. Open questions start with who, what, why, where, when, or how. This gets people talking rather than you having to make all the running.

6   Pay attention and be an active listener

- Your networking could be at a group event or on a 1 to 1 basis. These tips apply to both.
- If you are involved in a group conversation, and there is one person with whom you are interested in networking with, pay attention to everyone, don't just focus on the one you want to meet and ignore the others.
- You never know when something relevant to your needs will be mentioned. Keep focused on what is going on and keep your ears open.
- Allow others to talk. If there is no dialogue because you are doing all the talking you will not find out about the other person and if they do all the talking they will not find out about you.

- Remember, not everyone loves the sound of your voice!
- Be an active listener, nod and acknowledge what the other person is saying. Ask them open questions based on what they have just said.
- Don't appear to be half listening and over eager to move on. There is nothing more off putting to people than being in the company of someone who clearly wants to move on.

7   One on one networking is 100 times better than networking events

- Previously we have commented about the relative value of phone calls, webcam calls and face to face. We can now add the comparison between group events and one to one networking.
- Group events have the benefit of getting supposedly mutually interested people into the same place. However rarely does this work precisely, as people who are peripheral to where you want to be somehow get invited too.
- This means you can lose time by meeting people not relevant to your purpose for being there.
- The answer lies in the guest list that good networking event organisers produce, which at least allows you to earmark people you really do want to meet.
- Finally, be wary of events that you pay to attend. It is a balance about how much you will pay, against any web forum activities where previous visitors make good and bad comments.
- Consistently over the years one to one networking produces the best results.
- Sometimes these contacts come through someone you met at a networking event, mainly they come through those who you already know who introduce you to their contacts.

8   Handling phone or webcam networking

- Despite the face to face/one to one option, the next best option is a webcam or video conferencing.

- Avoid where you can, making a phone call as you completely miss out on the body language aspect which plays a key part of any human interface. Rarely have phone networking calls produced meaningful results.
- Today there are free web conferencing facilities where you can network via laptop, tablet or Smartphone.
- Even if your contact's organisation does not support the freely available conference call software, you should be able to see and speak to them via mobile phone or tablet.
- If usernames, passwords and setting up are required try to do this in advance to save your valuable networking time being taken up as one of you grapples with technology.

9   Responding to the needs of others

- Remember that this is not all about me, me, me!
- If you offer your help and advice to two or three people who approach you for networking advice, our expectation would be that you will get at least two to three names – up to nine or ten in total - resulting from the subsequent exchange of contacts.
- Your positive willingness to help will earmark you as a helpful person and others in an organisation are therefore more likely to offer to help you.
- You will also build on your "feel good factor" from helping others.

10 The follow up

- Here's a mistake that nine out of ten first time networkers make. We say to them "so how many networking meetings have you had?"
- They respond ".about 5 or 6". We say "that sounds good, how many names/contacts did you get from them?" The response is "oh, about 2 or 3"
- 'Dong' rings the alarm bell in our minds. They should be getting two to three contacts per meeting, so I should not be hearing "2 or 3", I should be hearing "between 12 and 18" Make sure you are growing a network – that's what the word means!
- Secondly having made one contact people think that's it – I have made contact.
- For effective networking results the ongoing contact should be either every 6 weeks or every 13 weeks.
- The **Learning Zone** at www.100toptips.com gives you a Contact Plan which allows you to list your growing contacts and set up a plan for regular contact.
- Another way to keep in contact in a positive way is giving the reader a short snappy email update of where you are and what you are doing. No more than three or four one liners in your email.
- The real advantage of this is that if you have 30 contacts to update it will only take you 20 minutes to send a personal email to all of them.
- We are giving you all the essential tools you need to follow up your networking.

Extract written by Ian Munro and from 100 + Top Tips for Developing Your Career

6   Chapter 10 – Heading

General Data Protection Regulation – GDPR

The General Data Protection Regulation (GDPR) came into effect on 25th May 2018. Whilst many are considering this the "doomsday" of marketing, it is in fact a straightforward process provided that you understand how to make your website GDPR compliant.

The motive behind the EU regulation is to protect consumers and customers against the rising data breaches, which is costing the UK economy billions of pounds a year. Several large firms have fallen victim to breaches.

The two key factors of the GDPR regulation are simple: keep customer data secure and make marketing communications as clear as possible. Failing to uphold these standards many result in a hefty fine which is has been lifted from 500,000 euros, to 20 million euros or 4% of annual turnover.

Thanks to www.techradar.com for this article.

7 Chapter 10 Tip 1

Invoicing log

NSG Invoice Log

Number	Client	Date	Detail	Expenses	V Excl	Vat	Total	Paid
3078	Masterflex	15-Nov	Consignment 2564		220.45	0.00	220.45	220.45
3079	Durable Ltd	20-Nov	Consignment 2568		162.22	32.44	194.66	
3080	M & S Supplies	20-Nov	Their PO 98566		328.72	0.00	328.72	
3081	Gardners	21-Nov	Consignment 2569		257.00	51.40	308.40	
3082	Rotors Ltd	25-Nov	Pro forma for therir PO ref DCL		85.66	0.00	85.66	26-Nov
3083	Ceruty	28-Nov	Consignment 2570	14.98	264.73	0.00	264.73	
3084						0.00	0.00	
3085						0.00	0.00	
3086						0.00	0.00	
3087						0.00	0.00	

Download at www.100toptips.com Learning Zone

`

8 Chapter 10 – Tip 3

Vat compilation form – see www.100toptips.com

Mar - May VAT Return
VAT @ 20%

INPUTS

MONTH	Chq	Date	Details	V.excl	Vat	Total
Mar to May	43	7-Mar	BT	299.17	59.83	359.00
				0.00	0.00	0.00
				0.00	0.00	0.00
				0.00	0.00	0.00
				0.00	0.00	0.00
				0.00	0.00	0.00
				0.00	0.00	0.00
				0.00	0.00	0.00
				0.00	0.00	0.00
				0.00	0.00	0.00
				0.00	0.00	0.00
				0.00	0.00	0.00
				0.00	0.00	0.00
				0.00	0.00	0.00
				0.00	0.00	0.00
				0.00	0.00	0.00
		Exs		390.22	30.29	420.51
Total				689.39	90.12	779.51

OUTPUTS

No.	Date	Details	V.excl	Vat	Total
2589	05-Mar	Joe Bloggs Ltd	1250.00	250.01	1500.00
2590	06-Mar	Marshot Ltd	2716.66	543.34	3260.00
			0.00	0.00	0.00
			416.67	83.34	500.00
			0.00	0.00	0.00
			0.00	0.00	0.00
			0.00	0.00	0.00
			0.00	0.00	0.00
			0.00	0.00	0.00
			0.00	0.00	0.00
			0.00	0.00	0.00
			0.00	0.00	0.00
			0.00	0.00	0.00
			0.00	0.00	0.00
			0.00	0.00	0.00
			0.00	0.00	0.00
			0.00	0.00	0.00
			0.00	0.00	0.00
			4383.32	876.68	5260.00

Less total input vat: -90.12

VAT due: 786.56

Note these fugures are linked to the expenses sheet

Qtr Expenses   VAT at 20%

M = Motor, Tr = Travel, O = Office and equipment, Sub = Subsistence

	Month				Month				Month		
	v. excl	vat	total		v. excl	vat	total		v. excl	vat	total
M	14.83	2.97	17.80	M	0.00	0.00	0.00	M	0.00	0.00	0.00
M	0.00	0.00	0.00	M	0.00	0.00	0.00	M	0.00	0.00	0.00
M	0.00	0.00	0.00	M	0.00	0.00	0.00	M	0.00	0.00	0.00
M	0.00	0.00	0.00	M	0.00	0.00	0.00	M	0.00	0.00	0.00
M	0.00	0.00	0.00	M	0.00	0.00	0.00	M	0.00	0.00	0.00
M	0.00	0.00	0.00	M	0.00	0.00	0.00	M	0.00	0.00	0.00
M	0.00	0.00	0.00	M	0.00	0.00	0.00	M	0.00	0.00	0.00
M	0.00	0.00	0.00	M	0.00	0.00	0.00	M	0.00	0.00	0.00
Tr	8.33	1.67	10.00	Tr	0.00	0.00	0.00	Tr	0.00	0.00	0.00
Tr	7.33	1.47	8.80	Tr	0.00	0.00	0.00	Tr	0.00	0.00	0.00
Tr	7.33	1.47	8.80	Tr	0.00	0.00	0.00	Tr	0.00	0.00	0.00
Tr	7.67	1.53	9.20	Tr	0.00	0.00	0.00	Tr	0.00	0.00	0.00
Tr	7.83	1.57	9.40	Tr	0.00	0.00	0.00	Tr	0.00	0.00	0.00
Tr	7.33	1.47	8.80	Tr	0.00	0.00	0.00	Tr	0.00	0.00	0.00
Tr	236.30	0.00	236.30	Tr	0.00	0.00	0.00	Tr	0.00	0.00	0.00
Tr	19.15	3.83	22.98	Tr	0.00	0.00	0.00	Tr	0.00	0.00	0.00
Tr	0.00	0.00	0.00	Tr	0.00	0.00	0.00	Tr	0.00	0.00	0.00
Tr	0.00	0.00	0.00	Tr	0.00	0.00	0.00	Tr	0.00	0.00	0.00
Tr	0.00	0.00	0.00	Tr	0.00	0.00	0.00	Tr	0.00	0.00	0.00
Tr	0.00	0.00	0.00	Tr	0.00	0.00	0.00	Tr	0.00	0.00	0.00
Tr	0.00	0.00	0.00	Tr	0.00	0.00	0.00	Tr	0.00	0.00	0.00
Tr	0.00	0.00	0.00	Tr	0.00	0.00	0.00	Tr	0.00	0.00	0.00
Tr	0.00	0.00	0.00	Tr	0.00	0.00	0.00	Tr	0.00	0.00	0.00
O	25.87	5.18	31.05	O	0.00	0.00	0.00	O	0.00	0.00	0.00
O	2.50	0.00	2.50	O	0.00	0.00	0.00	O	0.00	0.00	0.00
O	0.00	0.00	0.00	O	0.00	0.00	0.00	O	0.00	0.00	0.00
O	0.00	0.00	0.00	O	0.00	0.00	0.00	O	0.00	0.00	0.00
O	0.00	0.00	0.00	O	0.00	0.00	0.00	O	0.00	0.00	0.00
O	0.00	0.00	0.00	O	0.00	0.00	0.00	O	0.00	0.00	0.00
O	0.00	0.00	0.00	O	0.00	0.00	0.00	O	0.00	0.00	0.00
O	0.00	0.00	0.00	O	0.00	0.00	0.00	O	0.00	0.00	0.00
O	0.00	0.00	0.00	O	0.00	0.00	0.00	O	0.00	0.00	0.00
O	0.00	0.00	0.00	O	0.00	0.00	0.00	O	0.00	0.00	0.00
O	0.00	0.00	0.00	O	0.00	0.00	0.00	O	0.00	0.00	0.00
O	0.00	0.00	0.00	O	0.00	0.00	0.00	O	0.00	0.00	0.00
Sub	3.79	0.76	4.55	Sub	0.00	0.00	0.00	Sub	0.00	0.00	0.00
Sub	5.25	1.05	6.30	Sub	0.00	0.00	0.00	Sub	0.00	0.00	0.00
Sub	2.12	0.43	2.55	Sub	0.00	0.00	0.00	Sub	0.00	0.00	0.00
Sub	2.29	0.46	2.75	Sub	0.00	0.00	0.00	Sub	0.00	0.00	0.00
Sub	2.54	0.51	3.05	Sub	0.00	0.00	0.00	Sub	0.00	0.00	0.00
Sub	3.79	0.76	4.55	Sub	0.00	0.00	0.00	Sub	0.00	0.00	0.00
Sub	5.50	1.10	6.60	Sub	0.00	0.00	0.00	Sub	0.00	0.00	0.00
Sub	8.08	1.62	9.70	Sub	0.00	0.00	0.00	Sub	0.00	0.00	0.00
Sub	2.92	0.58	3.50	Sub	0.00	0.00	0.00	Sub	0.00	0.00	0.00
Sub	5.77	1.16	6.93	Sub	0.00	0.00	0.00	Sub	0.00	0.00	0.00
Sub	3.67	0.73	4.40	Sub	0.00	0.00	0.00	Sub	0.00	0.00	0.00
Sub	0.00	0.00	0.00	Sub	0.00	0.00	0.00	Sub	0.00	0.00	0.00
Sub	0.00	0.00	0.00	Sub	0.00	0.00	0.00	Sub	0.00	0.00	0.00
	390.22	30.29	420.51		0.00	0.00	0.00		0.00	0.00	0.00
M	14.83	2.97	17.80	M	0.00	0.00	0.00	M	0.00	0.00	0.00
Tr	301.28	13.00	314.28	Tr	0.00	0.00	0.00	Tr	0.00	0.00	0.00
O	28.37	5.18	33.55	O	0.00	0.00	0.00	O	0.00	0.00	0.00
Sub	45.73	9.15	54.88	Sub	0.00	0.00	0.00	Sub	0.00	0.00	0.00
Total	390.22	30.29	420.51	Total	0.00	0.00	0.00	Total	0.00	0.00	0.00

Qtr   390.22   30.29   420.51

Miles

Download at www.100toptips.com Learning Zone

INDEX

THIS FINALPAGE IS FOR YOUR LAST NOTES

Here is a final tip. If you lend this book to someone, put their name and date you lent it on this page. This may improve your chance of getting it back!

BV - #0025 - 131219 - C0 - 234/156/9 - PB - 9780993465857